THE BUSINESS OF DATA

This book is about the rise of data as a driver of innovation and economic growth. It charts the evolution of business data as a valuable resource and explores some of the key business, economic and social issues surrounding the data-driven revolution we are currently going through.

Readers will gain an understanding of the historical underpinnings of the data business and why the collection and use of data has been driven by commercial needs. Readers will also gain insights into the rise of the modern data-driven technology giants, their business models and the reasons for their success. Alongside this, some of the key social issues including privacy are considered and the challenges these pose to policymakers and regulators. Finally, the impact of pervasive computing and the Internet of Things (IoT) is explored in the context of the new sources of data that are being generated.

This book is useful for students and practitioners wanting to better understand the origins and drivers of the current technological revolution and the key role that data plays in innovation and business success.

Martin De Saulles is a Principal Lecturer at the University of Brighton, UK, teaching courses on innovation, marketing and business strategy.

INNOVATION AND TECHNOLOGY HORIZONS

Series Editor: **Vanessa Ratten**, *La Trobe University, Australia*

As business landscape constantly shifts in today's digital age, this timely series looks at how business and society can harness technological innovation to succeed and drive progress. The books in this series identify new innovation capabilities and emerging technologies and investigate the managerial implications of such technologies. As business processes become increasingly complex, the series also explores how businesses can transform themselves with new digital technologies while aligning themselves with today's societal goals. This series provides direction through research on innovation and technology management and will be of benefit to anyone who is keen to thrive in an evolving business environment.

Tourism Innovation
Technology, Sustainability and Creativity
Edited by Vanessa Ratten, Vitor Braga, José Álvarez Garcia and Maria de la Cruz del Rio-Rama

Social Innovation
Asian Case Studies of Innovating for the Common Good
Edited by Sarah Lai-Yin Cheah

Tourism, Hospitality and Digital Transformation
Strategic Management Aspects
Edited by Kayhan Tajeddini, Vanessa Ratten and Thorsten Merkle

Managing Sustainable Innovation
Edited by Vanessa Ratten, Marcela Ramirez-Pasillas and Hans Lundberg

The Business of Data
Commercial Opportunities and Social Challenges in a World Fuelled by Data
Martin De Saulles

For more information about this series, please visit www.routledge.com/ Innovation-and-Technology-Horizons/book-series/ITH

THE BUSINESS OF DATA

Commercial Opportunities and Social Challenges in a World Fuelled by Data

Martin De Saulles

LONDON AND NEW YORK

First published 2021
by Routledge
2 Park Square, Milton Park, Abingdon, Oxon OX14 4RN

and by Routledge
52 Vanderbilt Avenue, New York, NY 10017

Routledge is an imprint of the Taylor & Francis Group, an informa business

© 2021 Martin De Saulles

The right of Martin De Saulles to be identified as author of this work has been
asserted by him in accordance with sections 77 and 78 of the Copyright,
Designs and Patents Act 1988.

All rights reserved. No part of this book may be reprinted or reproduced or utilised
in any form or by any electronic, mechanical, or other means, now known or
hereafter invented, including photocopying and recording, or in any information
storage or retrieval system, without permission in writing from the publishers.

Trademark notice: Product or corporate names may be trademarks or registered trademarks,
and are used only for identification and explanation without intent to infringe.

British Library Cataloguing-in-Publication Data
A catalogue record for this book is available from the British Library

Library of Congress Cataloging-in-Publication Data
Names: De Saulles, Martin, author.
Title: The business of data: commercial opportunities and social
challenges in a world fuelled by data / Martin De Saulles.
Description: Abingdon, Oxon; New York, NY: Routledge, 2020. |
Series: Innovation and technology horizons |
Includes bibliographical references and index.
Identifiers: LCCN 2020009556 (print) | LCCN 2020009557 (ebook)
Subjects: LCSH: Information technology–Economic aspects. |
Big data–Economic aspects. | Business intelligence. |
Technological innovations–Economic aspects.
Classification: LCC HC79.I55 D42 2020 (print) |
LCC HC79.I55 (ebook) | DDC 658/.0557–dc23
LC record available at https://lccn.loc.gov/2020009556
LC ebook record available at https://lccn.loc.gov/2020009557

ISBN: 978-1-138-38566-5 (hbk)
ISBN: 978-1-138-38567-2 (pbk)
ISBN: 978-0-429-42702-2 (ebk)

Typeset in Bembo
by Newgen Publishing UK

For Jerome

CONTENTS

1	Introduction	1
2	Origins of business data	3
3	Data generation and use in the twenty-first century: the rise of the new data monopolies	21
4	Emerging business models of data-driven companies	45
5	Challenges for policymakers and law makers: privacy in a world of data	59
6	Pervasive computing and data futures	83
7	Conclusion	109
	Index	*113*

1

INTRODUCTION

We are increasingly told that we are now living in an information society, that data is the new oil or that big data is going to change the world. It is certainly true that we have never been surrounded by so much data, much of it generated by our everyday activities. Scarcely a day goes by without another news story about another data breach suffered by companies and governments, either through human error or as the result of determined hackers. However, the story behind why this data was created in the first place and how it is used by businesses and public organisations to make profits or improve our daily lives is less frequently told. This book attempts to answer these questions and show that data has become an integral part of all developed economies, driving innovation and fuelling industries. As long as humans have engaged in commerce, the capture, storage, processing and exchange of data has been a vital element in the transaction process. Over the last 100 years it has also become an industry in its own right. In the last 20 years this industry has grown to the extent that many of the world's largest and most profitable companies are essentially data-driven entities. Appreciating these changes and the driving forces behind them is essential for anyone wanting to understand business in the twenty-first century.

Chapter 2 considers the history of data from a business perspective and traces its origins back to the earliest known forms of writing. It then traces the evolution of data as business resource from the first stock exchanges of the eighteenth century, through the rise of managerialism in the early twentieth century up to the post-war computing era.

In Chapter 3, the rise of the internet and the companies spawned from this digital revolution are explored with the distinct phases of this period explained. It shows how the capture and exploitation of data emanating from internet users has been central to the rise of the internet giants we know today. These companies and

2 Introduction

their data strategies are considered in the context of the different business models each of the companies has developed.

Chapter 4 goes into more detail on data-driven business models, their configuration and the trends emerging from a maturing internet economy. The economics of information and how they differ from the economic forces governing more traditional business assets are explored in the context of innovation.

The rapidly developing challenges facing regulators and policymakers are described in Chapter 5 and recent examples of data misuse are highlighted to illustrate this growing problem. Just as data presents new opportunities and challenges for business to exploit, so regulators are faced with a highly fluid and complex landscape where the use of data requires legislation to protect individuals in the same way as the financial sector.

Finally, in Chapter 6 the future of computing is considered with a focus on pervasive computing and the Internet of Things (IoT) and the implications of this wave of innovation for data both from a business perspective and a social one. As computing becomes more embedded in our daily lives and the data these new technologies generates becomes the driving force for their deployment, data will emerge as a defining resource of the twenty-first century. As this chapter illustrates, it can be used to transform our work and social lives as well as our personal health but stricter controls will be needed to ensure the balance between the demands of business and the privacy of individuals is secured at an appropriate level.

2

ORIGINS OF BUSINESS DATA

Some of the earliest records we have of writing and notation were created to record business transactions and financial accounts. Going back thousands of years, wherever goods and money changed hands there were often tools available to note these exchanges and, in a few cases, these records still exist. In 1929, Julius Jordan, a German archaeologist, discovered a trove of clay tablets over 5,000 years old in what is now Iraq. For nearly 50 years the markings on the tablets were a mystery until it was discovered they had been created to record the receipt and then sale of commodities such as grain, sheep and honey. What had been thought by many historians and archaeologists to be early forms of poetry and personal correspondence were actually accounts created to provide a note of what had been bought, how much had been paid and what was still owed (Harford, 2017). As these tablets and tokens were studied further it became clear that they were more sophisticated than originally thought. Recording the sale of four sheep involved the sheep symbol being pressed four times into the clay but larger transactions would take up too much space so a shortened set of symbols were created where a circle represented ten and other symbols indicated larger amounts, allowing large numbers into the thousands to be represented. According to Harford (2017), one of the tablets recorded a demand for war reparations amounting to 4.5 trillion litres of barley, approximately 600 times the current annual US production of barley.

Over time these records grew more sophisticated and by 1,800 BC in Babylon the so-called Code of Hammurabi was in use, which formalised the first known rules around the granting of credit. The code set the maximum amounts of interest that could be charged with, for example, loans on grain having a limit of 33.3% per year and silver 20%. For these transactions and loans to have legal weight, they had to be witnessed by a public official and formally recorded as a contract (Desjardins, 2017). Credit notes were extensively used in ancient Rome, with Cicero noting in 50 BC that his neighbour had recently purchased 625 acres of land for 11.5 million

4 Origins of business data

sesterces. As Desjardins (2017) notes, that number of sesterces would weight more than 11 tonnes and be an unfeasibly large amount of coin to transport through the streets of Rome. Therefore, the transaction would have relied on a formal credit note to complete the purchase.

European explorers and the resulting colonial expansion into the Americas, Africa and Asia stimulated the need for credit to fund these expensive forays and the modern banking industry started to take shape. By the nineteenth century a growing middle class in many industrialised economies extended the rise of credit to individuals, requiring data gathering and processing on an unprecedented scale. This continued to grow throughout the twentieth century up to the present day and now forms a cornerstone of the financial data sector.

As business's reliance on data gathering and processing grew, so did the tools and techniques to help them in this process. Access to data, particularly in the financial markets, could prove a significant competitive advantage for companies that were able to have sight of commodity prices or significant news before their rivals. News reporting services such as Reuters and stock market data feeds emerged to fill this demand for information and the business data sector started to take shape. A core task for any business is the ability to make informed decisions based on experience but also using relevant data as a core input in this process. As trade and commerce has expanded throughout the previous 200 years across developed economies, systems have been required to ensure companies can be paid for their products and services. What started in Mesopotamia over 5,000 years ago with clay tablets has now evolved into a multi-trillion-dollar industry underpinning how we work and live. The following sections in this chapter will explore how new technologies such as the printing press, telecommunication networks and computing have been both drivers of innovation in the business of data as well as having been shaped themselves by the collection, storage and exploitation of data. Human activities in public and private spheres leave traces which are recorded for a variety of legal and commercial reasons and have a monetary value of their own. The ingenuity of individuals to create profitable enterprises around these data streams will become apparent, as will the social challenges that arise from this activity.

The rise of the printing press

As we have seen, the formal notation of information into clay tablets and later manuscripts made from papyrus, velum and paper can be traced back thousands of years. However, one of the key limiting features of such techniques and media is the time-consuming nature of their production. Each must be written by hand, restricting the uses to which recorded data can be put and the types of people given access to it. The rise of the printing press began a radical transformation in the volume and types of printed materials which could be produced. Early printing presses typically relied on carved wooden panels to be painted with ink and compressed against printable media in a process known as block printing. While more efficient than handwriting for the 'mass' production of information, block

Origins of business data **5**

printing is limited by the nature of the wooden panels only being able to print the same text or illustration each time they are used.

At the end of the first millennium AD the first moveable-type printing press was developed in China where individual carved letters could be set and re-used, allowing a much faster and more flexible system of printing. In the fifteenth century in Germany, Johannes Gutenberg developed the concept of moveable type and replaced the wooden letters with metal ones. Incremental innovations to Gutenberg's printing press were made by fellow German Peter Schoffer, whose version of *The Book of Psalms* incorporated a three-colour title page.

While the more rapid and accurate printing of books and other documents made possible by the moveable-type printing press led to a vibrant printing industry across much of Europe, it is the social, political and economic implications which are most interesting. Less expensive and therefore more books meant ideas could be spread far quicker than previously, and this proved a challenge to those in power, particularly the Church. Pope Alexander VI decreed in 1501 that anyone printing texts without the Church's approval would be excommunicated. This threat to the authority of the Catholic hierarchy was realised a few years later, when books by Martin Luther and John Calvin split the Church and fragmented the power of religious authorities.

As ideas spread so people began to question many perceived truths, and not just within the religious realms. The so-called Age of Enlightenment was fuelled by the ability of scholars to share information and knowledge and the origins of science as a discipline emerged. According to Rayward (2014):

> Of central importance in understanding the emergence of the Gutenberg-based information and communications infrastructures and what these infrastructures supported was the fact that they were an integral part of the general secularization, modernization, and industrialization of Western capitalist economies.
>
> *(Rayward, 2014, pp. 682–683)*

The mass production of printed materials went hand-in-hand with the origins of the Industrial Revolution across much of Europe. As economic activity grew with the move from agricultural to industrial development, so the need for enhanced record keeping also increased. Industrial methods and innovation were also applied to the printing press itself with the development of new steam-powered machines and rotary presses that could print millions of copies of a page in a day. At this scale, it became possible to print mass-distribution newspapers and, coupled with the rise of railways in the mid-nineteenth century, the national press was born.

As books became cheaper to produce and systems of education were developed in many industrialised economies, reading moved from being a luxury for the rich or those in religious orders to a mass pursuit. Book publishers catering for all tastes began to flourish and a new industry emerged.

6 Origins of business data

Many of the origins of the data business can be traced back to the era of mass printing. For the first time information was not a scarce resource guarded by the chosen few but was becoming a common good available to almost anyone. Entrepreneurs were quick to spot the potential for building businesses around this new resource. Newspaper publishers realised the profits that could be made through charging pennies for each copy but also then selling their readers' attention to advertisers desperate to promote their products to a growing middle class. Directory publishers found a profitable niche in providing printed guides to local businesses and book publishers found a ready market for novels of all types.

This emerging industry for printed materials of all types also played an important part in the transformation of how businesses were managed as record keeping emerged as a distinct practice and more formalised management techniques began to be applied across the industrial landscape.

Managerialism and record keeping

The application of 'scientific' methods to the management and organising of business operations started to take hold in the early twentieth century as larger companies expanded their operations across ever-wider geographic areas and employed many thousands of people in factory and office settings. Controlling these sprawling businesses to ensure profits were being maximised was a challenge and the rise of mass production, particularly in the automotive sector, only accelerated this problem.

A founding father of scientific management was F.W. Taylor (1911), who relied on the rise of record keeping to underpin his ideas on how a workplace should be run.

> Under the best day work of the ordinary type, when accurate records are kept of the amount of work done by each man and of his efficiency ... And this one best method and best implement can only be discovered or developed through a scientific study and analysis of all of the methods and implements in use, together with accurate, minute, motion and time study.
>
> *(Taylor, 1911, p. 8)*

Taylor's work, as well as that of other pioneers of scientific management techniques such as Frank Gilbreth and Harrington Emerson, applied formal methodologies including time and motion studies of workers to the process and organisation of work and working practices. These techniques relied on careful monitoring and record keeping which generated new classes of business information that needed to be stored in ways that allowed ready access for managers and administrators. At the same time, innovations in the technologies for creating, storing and retrieving information were developed with a raft of devices taken up by businesses including typewriters, telephones, stencil duplicators, accounting machines, filing cabinets and index cards (Black, 2006). Later came more sophisticated technologies such as punch-card machines, photostats and microfilm readers.

It could be said that the first half of the twentieth century in most industrialised economies saw the formalisation of work in terms of processes which relied on the systematic collection and manipulation of data. These new techniques of management were given a boost during the Second World War in the US as information management became a core function of the war effort. Coordinating the massive public and private investments in the production of materials and supplies needed to equip an army as well as the logistics of mobilising millions of civilians to fight and work in the factories required managing unprecedented volumes of information. A key figure in these efforts was Vannevar Bush, appointed to lead the US Office of Scientific Research and Development in 1941. A core part of his work was to ensure that information was shared effectively between branches of the military and other organisations that needed it to support the war effort. His focus on information management led Bush to develop the concept of what he called a memex machine. The objective of the machine was to help researchers and managers augment their memory capabilities through the use of microfilm that could store the contents of books, journals and records. Central to the concept was the linking of data by association rather than the established practices of using indexes and hierarchical filing systems. He was aware that the human brain did not work in the same way as information management systems of the time and that something was needed to allow the speedy and efficient retrieval of data based on concepts and not rigid catalogues. Although the machine was never built, the idea behind it came to fruition 50 years later with the World Wide Web (WWW).

The business of financial and credit data

Companies spent $168 billion on financial, credit and compliance data and associated services in 2016 according to Watson Healy (2017). While this data underpins the modern global banking and financial sector, its origins can be found in early-seventeenth-century Amsterdam and the first financial markets. At the time shares in the newly founded Dutch East India Company were being traded in multiple venues across Amsterdam offering opportunities for traders with access to the most recent data on share transactions to buy and sell company stock knowing more than their competitors about the market. Known as arbitrage, this approach to trading still takes place today and rests on a trader knowing something that the other party to the transaction does not. In Amsterdam 500 years ago information networks emerged to share this data in mutually beneficial ways to network members (Donnan, 2011).

Similar networks emerged in other cities around the world with the London Stock Exchange emerging from an information sharing club formed by 150 men in 1761 and something similar emerging in New York in 1792 (Donnan, 2011). Volumes of shares being traded were very low by modern standards and so rudimentary paper-based systems were adequate to track transactions and prices.

8 Origins of business data

Pricing data was particularly time-sensitive as access offered substantial arbitrage opportunities. In the early nineteenth century, German Paul Julius Reuter used carrier pigeons to fly stock prices between markets in Aachen and Brussels and in 1851 he opened an office in London to transmit stock market data between London and Paris over the newly laid Dover–Calais cable (Reuters, 2008). Efforts to gain time advantages over trading rivals continue to this day through massive investments in communication networks. In 2010, Spread Networks invested $300 million to drill through mountains in a project to lay a 827-mile-long fibre-optic cable between Chicago and New York. Even though this cable only shaved four-thousandths of a second off the existing transmission time for this route, financial institutions were still willing to spend tens of millions of dollars to access the data (Lewis, 2015). Even more ambitious is SpaceX's Starlink project to launch 12,000 satellites into space at a cost of over $10 billion to allow high-speed internet connections across the globe. While this may help connect remote parts of the world to the internet, an initial objective of the project is to provide faster connections with lower latency rates to financial institutions for the exchange of time-sensitive market data (Chang, 2019).

Another type of financial data central to the modern banking system is credit information. We have seen how credit notes recording transactions and logging who owes what to whom have been used for thousands of years but the modern credit information industry can be traced back to the early nineteenth century. In 1803 a group of London tailors began sharing information about customers who had not paid their bills. This data became valuable not only to the tailors keen to avoid bad debts but also to other institutions wanting to know how credit-worthy potential customers might be. Minimising the risk of loan defaults is a central part of the operation of banks and data on who could be trusted to pay their debts became a valuable commodity. In 1826, the Society of Guardians for the Protection of Tradesmen and Swindlers was formed in Manchester and members received a monthly newsletter with information on people who had not paid their bills (Watson, 2013).

The demand for credit data grew rapidly in the early twentieth century on both sides of the Atlantic and in the US, by the 1920s, more than a fifth of purchases made in department stores were on credit, leading to the creation of over 1,000 credit agencies (Watson, 2013). The post-Second World War consumer spending boom accelerated this trend to the extent that the global market for credit data was worth almost $13 billion in 2016 (Watson Healy, 2017). As credit agencies grew in number and size, so did the types of data they collected to ascertain credit scores for individuals. By the 1950s in the US, agencies were scouring local newspapers for news on promotions, arrests, marriages and deaths as it was all data that could help determine the propensity of someone to pay their bills on time (Desjardins, 2017). The application of computing technologies to the industry from the 1960s formed the basis for the industry we know today where standardised methodologies such as the FICO score are used to combine data on amounts owed, payment history and credit mix. Credit agencies such as Experian have also found ways to persuade individuals to pay for information about their own credit scores via smartphone apps.

The rise of mass media and marketing

The first mass media were newspapers, whose existence can be traced back to the seventeenth century with the *Oxford Gazette*. However, it was not until the nineteenth century with the rise of railways to transport them and improved industrial presses to print them that newspapers became a prime source of information and entertainment for the general population. The earliest newspapers were based on a business model that relied on the cover price or subscription rate to generate revenues. However, in 1833 in New York, a print shop owner, Benjamin Day, wondered if there was a market for a paper that would be affordable for the masses. At the time the city was served by several newspapers, with the most popular costing 6 cents and having a circulation of 2,600 (Wu, 2016). At the time 6 cents was a significant amount of money and the paper was bought by business professionals to find out what had been going on in the world of commerce. Day's plan was to sell his newspaper at a loss for 1 cent and make up the profits by selling advertising space in each edition. Papers had been carrying advertising for a number of years but Day's paper would go for a mass audience enticed by the low cover price and then sell the attention of the large numbers of readers to marketers. The *New York Sun* was launched on 3 September 1833 and within several months was selling thousands of copies a day; within a year the losses incurred by the printing costs were more than offset by advertising revenue. With this the origins of a mass media and, by design, a mass-marketing industry started to take shape. By 1910 in the US, more than 2,200 daily newspapers were printed and read by over 20 million (Graham, 2000).

Throughout the twentieth century, radio and then television also became platforms for targeting marketing messages at mass audiences. As with newspapers, content for these media was primarily designed to attract large audiences as these were the most profitable to sell to advertisers. By 1930, radio advertising in the US was generating $60 million annually and this rose to $600 million by 1940 (the equivalent of $11 billion in 2019) (Graham, 2000). The rise of television advertising was even more dramatic than radio as the multimedia platform appealed more to consumers but also provided a richer platform for crafting marketing messages. Even by 2018 when digital marketing was taking an ever-larger share of advertising budgets, approximately $70 billion was being spent on television advertisements in the US (eMarketer, 2018).

Central to the ability of newspapers and radio and television channels to sell advertising is the data they use to demonstrate to marketers who is consuming their media and in what volumes. Audience measurement systems have evolved over the previous 100 years but, for traditional media, still tend to rely on samples and audience panels to estimate viewing figures. The nature of broadcast media such

10 Origins of business data

as terrestrial radio and television is that broadcasters do not know who is tuning in to their channels as there is no way of measuring this. As a result, television audiences are calculated using set-top boxes installed in a representative sample of homes and remote controls whereby individuals in the household can log when they are watching a particular programme. While this is an imperfect system, it is an agreed methodology that advertisers and media owners broadly trust. As systems for measuring audiences developed, so did techniques for performing market research to ascertain public opinions on particular products, brands and advertising messages. From its origins in the early twentieth century when 100 members of the Advertising Club of New York met for the first talk on the role of market research in advertising (Lockley, 1950), the business of gathering opinions and data on tastes was worth nearly $40 billion in 2016 (Watson Healy, 2017).

While mass marketing has historically relied on sample data and best estimates of audience size, direct marketing has its roots in the use of personal data to target consumers. Direct marketing at scale began in nineteenth-century America when catalogue publishers built up relationships with consumers who were spread across the vast country and often not within easy reach of a store. In the 1880s, Sears launched its catalogue and within ten years the 500-page tome was being sent to more than 300,000 homes (Sears, 2012). In the 1950s, the term 'direct marketing' was coined by Lester Wunderman, the founder of the first agency dedicated to this activity, who realised that the data held by catalogue companies about their customers could be used to market other products and services to them. The collection and analysis of consumer data is central to successful direct marketing approaches as the focus is on accurate targeting of messages at specific individuals rather than the more scattergun approach of mass media marketing. This data-driven approach has now evolved into a far more sophisticated set of activities used by digital marketers who have unprecedented volumes as well as precise data to play with.

The origins of electronic communications

When charting a timeline for the evolution of data as a valuable commodity, the rise of electronic networks in the nineteenth century formed the foundation for what is often referred to as the Information Age. We have already seen how the demand for timely financial data on stock market activity led to massive investments, first in the electronic telegraph in the 1860s, *with The Wall Street Journal* proudly announcing in 1889 that:

> Today it takes less than 30 seconds for the price of the latest trade to travel the 216 miles between the Boston Stock Exchange and the NYSE. From almost anywhere in the US with telegraph service, an order can be sent to New York and confirmation of the executed trade received back in less than 90 seconds. Trades cross the Atlantic in under five minutes.
>
> *(Zweig, 2014)*

As is the case in most areas of human activity, where there is something of value there will be someone trying to dishonestly make a profit from it. The telegraph was no exception. Early telegraph fraud centred on transmitting the results of horse races to towns many miles away from the racecourse so that punters could place bets on races knowing who the winner was before the bookmakers had access to the same information. Similar scams involving the sending of stock market data from London to Edinburgh were undertaken by stockbrokers until the fraud was detected (Standage, 1999).

The telephone followed later in the century and for the first 100 years was primarily used for voice communications. However, dedicated networks built to transport data primarily for business customers were deployed in the second half of the twentieth century with new protocols such as packet switching developed to more efficiently route data across dispersed systems. However, it was the rise of the internet from the late 1990s that saw telecommunication networks become focused more on data transmission than voice communications. Information that up till then had been primarily transmitted across wireless broadcast networks for entertainment purposes could now pass across the wires of the telephone companies, offering new revenue streams for them and new opportunities to make money from data for other businesses. Central to this revolution was the digitisation of data from analogue signals to a stream of 0s and 1s which could be decoded as a perfect copy at the receiving end. Just as the telegraph broke down the limitations of geography on transporting messages for the first time, so did the internet and its associated protocols for sending and receiving information revolutionise the data business.

The computing age

The internet and the WWW allowed Bush's notion of a memex machine to become reality. Underpinning this revolution was the mass deployment of computing technologies and devices which permitted the digital coding and decoding of data at each end of the network in a way that the microfilm media suggested by Bush for the memex could never have done.

Automated manipulation of data can be traced back to the early nineteenth century when Semen Korsakov, a Russian statistician, invented a way of accessing information stored on punch cards that had previously been used to control textile looms. Several years later the British mathematician Charles Babbage outlined how he might use these cards to input data into his analytical engine. In the late nineteenth century another statistician, the American Herman Hollerith, devised an electro-mechanical tabulating machine which was used to process data from the 1890 US census. Its benefits over manual data processing were evident when it reduced the time taken to process census data from eight years to one. It is often claimed that the age of modern data processing began with Hollerith's machine (Wylie et al., 2013). His company later merged with several other firms to become International Business Machines (IBM) in 1924.

12 Origins of business data

From the 1930s advances in data processing were given a boost by the US government when it contracted IBM to build a system capable of holding employment records of 26 million working Americans and 3 million employees (Wylie et al., 2013). The Second World War accelerated this process and efforts in the UK to crack encrypted German messages resulted in the world's first programmable electronic computer, Colossus, capable of reading paper tape at 5,000 characters per second.

After the war, advances in data storage saw the rise of magnetic storage, first with magnetic tape from Remington Rand in the US in 1951 and five years later with magnetic discs from IBM. As corporations started to realise the benefits of data management at scale to their operations, the notion of 'business intelligence' as a focus of activity emerged in the late 1950s and the invention of relational databases a decade or so later transformed how complex datasets could be managed. Retailers and large consumer goods companies led this revolution as tracking sales through scanning data allowed much more efficient supply chains. By the early 1990s data warehouses started to be built as ways to store and process the massive amounts of data being generated by automated supply chains and business processes, with the term 'big data' first being used in 1997.

The rise of the information economy

While economists, policymakers and journalists now talk frequently about the central role of communications technologies and data in modern economies, it is important to remember that these are not new discussions. In the late eighteenth century the economist and philosopher Adam Smith was writing about the importance of new technologies and ways of working in the shaping of the emerging industrial British economy.

> Thirdly, and lastly, everybody must be sensible how much labour is facilitated and abridged by the application of proper machinery … A part of the machines made use of in those manufactures in which labour is subdivided, were originally the inventions of common workmen, who, being each of them employed in some very simple operation, naturally turned their thoughts towards finding out easier and readier methods of performing it.
>
> *(Smith, 1986, p. 114)*

One hundred and fifty years later, the Russian economist Nikolai Kondratiev observed the phenomena of long waves of economic growth and decline across industrialised economies which was picked up by Austrian economist Joseph Schumpeter a few years later, who termed these cycles Kondratiev Waves. Schumpeter's contribution to this debate on economic growth was his hypothesis that these cycles were the result of waves of continuous innovation and what he called 'creative destruction'. Major innovations, in Schumpeter's view, had the power to transform economies and stimulate economic growth while at the same

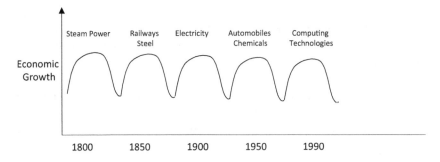

FIGURE 2.1 Kondratiev Cycles

time destroying many established ways of work and production. These long waves of economic growth and decline could take approximately 50 years to play out and, according to post-Schumpeterian scholars, can be divided into five cycles, each stimulated by the arrival and deployment of a new and disruptive wave of innovations. Figure 2.1 illustrates this.

As can be seen in Figure 2.1, it was industrial innovations which drove the first four waves of economic growth across these Kondratiev Waves. Their impact was felt largely through the industrialisation of Western economies, accompanied by the mass production of goods and the rise of the consumer society. The fifth wave, which many would argue we are still experiencing, has been driven by information and communication technologies over the previous several decades and the application of computing to our work and social lives. While industrialisation saw the rise of mass-produced and affordable goods for many people, this fifth wave could be characterised by the volumes of data it is generating.

The rise of data generation as a by-product of the application of computing technologies and, more recently, as an input to new products and services has been commented on by many social scientists over the previous 50 years. The business historian Alfred D. Chandler has written extensively about the transformation of work through the rise of new technologies and, in the tradition of Schumpeter, talks of stages of evolution which industrialised economies have gone through: the Commercial Age, the Industrial Age and the Information Age (Chandler and Cortada, 2000). The Information Age, he argues, took hold in the latter part of the twentieth century as new information and communication technologies were embedded in the working practices of modern businesses and information processing became a core function for many firms. This builds on the quantitative research carried out by Fritz Machlup (1962) and his mapping of the information industries in the US in the early 1960s. Machlup was aware of the rising importance of information processing technologies and the new types of companies and resulting roles for workers in this new age. A few years later, Marc Uri Porat (1977) performed a similar piece of research to Machlup's and provided statistics for the extent of the deployment of new technologies within the US. The title of his report, 'The Information Economy: Definition and Measurement', indicates the acceptance of the concept of the central role of information to economic activity and growth. Also significant is Porat's attempt to define what is meant by the terms 'data' and 'information'.

> Information is data that have been organized and communicated. The information activity includes all the resources, consumed in producing, processing and distributing information goods and services.
>
> *(Porat, 1977, p. 2)*

The notion of a difference between data and information is important and has been taken up and developed by later researchers and writers. Later definitions have also included the idea of 'knowledge' and, even more recently, 'wisdom'. These differences are often described as a form of value chain where an evolutionary process occurs which turns data into wisdom. Figure 2.2 illustrates this process.

To simplify, data can be seen as the raw material which is generated through activities that can be collected and stored by computing technologies. For example data might be the outputs of a weather monitoring station or statistics from a marketing survey. Information can be created from this data when it is interpreted and meaning applied to it which can be understood by those using it. This first round of processing can be performed by humans or machines. Turning information into knowledge is a more complex process that draws on experience and has been the preserve of people with expertise in the given area to perform. Enthusiastic claims for 'knowledge management' systems made by technology firms in the late 1990s

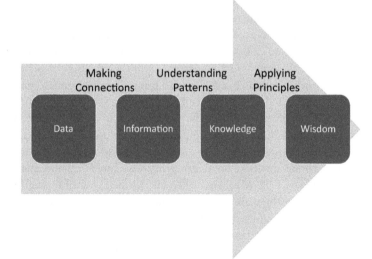

FIGURE 2.2 Data into knowledge

and early 2000s offered hope that this stage too could be automated. However, these claims were often unrealistic and in many cases considered nonsensical (Wilson, 2002). Wisdom is even more difficult to pin down as a definition but tends to relate to the ability of human interpreters of information/knowledge to arrive at decisions based more on instinct than methodical reasoning. It is possible that recent and ongoing advances in artificial intelligence (AI) may provide practical tools and techniques for the automated generation of knowledge insights into data. The challenge of programming driverless cars to cope with the vagaries of the road network and the behaviour of other drivers and pedestrians may prove a vital step in this process.

Data as the new oil

Just as the refining of oil into petroleum drove a large part of the economic growth of the industrialised world in the twentieth century, so many commentators have predicted that data will be the new oil for the current century. Industries, it is argued, will be built on the gathering, processing and exploitation of data as we move away from our industrial past. As put in a recent article in *The Economist*, titled 'The World's Most Valuable Resource is No Longer Oil but Data':

> This abundance of data changes the nature of competition ... By collecting more data, a firm has more scope to improve its products, which attracts more users, generating even more data, and so on. The more data Tesla gathers from its self-driving cars, the better it can make them at driving themselves—part of the reason the firm, which sold only 25,000 cars in the first quarter, is now worth more than GM, which sold 2.3m. Vast pools of data can thus act as protective moats.
>
> *(The Economist, 2017)*

We shall return to the potential competitive advantages that data exploitation offers through network effects later in this book but it is important to note here how data is increasingly seen as a core resource rather than just a by-product of other activities.

Mapping this data revolution presents challenges as the landscape is changing rapidly as new technologies and services are adopted at increasing speed. In the US and UK it took approximately 100 years for more than 90% of households to have a telephone. PCs did not appear on most people's desks until almost 50 years after the invention of the computer. However, in most developed economies more than 80% of adults had internet access at home within 20 years of the technology becoming widely available (Meeker, 2019). Ten years after the launch of the iPhone in 2007, three-quarters of UK adults owned a smartphone (Ofcom, 2018).

There are two broad numbers that researchers and analysts attempt to measure with respect to the information economy: the monetary value of the sector and

16 Origins of business data

the volume of data it generates. Quantifying these figures is difficult as data generating technologies and activities are spread across all sectors of the economy and embedded in our work and private lives. Unlike the production of automobiles or agricultural produce where public-sector bodies play a part in measuring activity for planning and tax purposes, the dispersed nature of technology producers and usage of their services are not centrally monitored. However, despite these problems a number of researchers have attempted to map the data universe.

In terms of the value of the 'information industries', in 2017 Thirani and Gupta (2017) at the World Economic Forum calculated that the global data economy was valued at $3 trillion. This is a rather vague figure and Watson Healy (2017) at consulting firm Outsell has been more precise in her estimation, with a figure of $1.6 trillion for 2016 broken down into the core industry sectors that generate and sell information-based products and services. In their study on the value generated through the collection and selling of personal data in the US alone, Shapiro and Aneja (2019) have calculated a figure of $76 billion for 2018. They make the interesting comparison that in the same year, US agriculture contributed $157 billion to the economy and predict that by 2022 the value of Americans' personal information will surpass the total value of agricultural production for that year.

Estimates for the volumes of data being generated through new information and communication technologies have been ongoing for a number of decades. In the late 1990s and early 2000s the rise of the internet and personal computing prompted a series of major studies at the University of California at Berkeley (Lyman and Varian, 2000, 2003). A core focus of their studies was on recordable media such as CD-ROMs, hard-disc drives and magnetic tape. More recently the focus has been on data stored on smartphones and cloud computing services as well as the millions of servers operated by technology giants such as Facebook, Google, Microsoft and Amazon.

A leading company in this area has been the consulting and research firm IDC. In 2018 it calculated that the Global Datasphere, as it terms the technologies generating and storing data, was 33 Zettabytes (ZB) in size and will grow to 175 ZB by 2025 (Reinsel et al., 2018). To put this into something approaching an understandable context, IDC provides the following example.

> If you could download the entire 2025 Global Datasphere at an average of 25 Mb/s, today's average connection speed across the United States, then it would take one person 1.8 billion years to do it, or if every person in the world could help and never rest, then you could get it done in 81 days.
>
> *(Reinsel et al., 2018, p. 7)*

While the total amount of data being generated and stored is impressive in terms of scale, it is important to note where the data is coming from and to make some distinctions between original data and copied data. IDC identifies three main types of information with respect to where it is stored:

1. core data – this includes data stored in computing datacentres and cloud computing providers;
2. edge data – this refers to data stored on corporate servers and smaller datacentres;
3. endpoint data – this is the data we are more familiar with and includes the data on our PCs, smartphones, wearables, industrial sensors and connected cars.

A trend in data storage over the previous decade has been a migration of much data that resided on consumer devices and commercial computers over to cloud computing providers. As fixed and mobile broadband connections become faster and more ubiquitous and multiple computing devices become the norm, it is more convenient for end users to access the data they need from remote servers. This goes hand-in-hand with a growing demand for access to real-time data by consumers and businesses. In industrial settings the growth of embedded sensors across factories and in machinery is generating large volumes of data in real time. At a personal level IDC calculates that by 2025 every connected person on the planet will have an average of 4,900 digital data engagements per day. These would include checking social media feeds, email, news alerts, instant messaging and so on.

Another distinction to make is between original data and copies of that data. For example, where a cloud computing provider such as Google Drive or Microsoft's OneDrive is used to keep synchronised backups of data created on PCs and smartphones there will be at least one copy of all the original files that are created. Similarly, most organisations will have a formal policy of backing up files and data to remote servers in case of data loss. It has been estimated that the ratio of replicated to original data is approximately 8:1 (Meeker, 2019).

Later chapters will explore in more detail the commercial and policy implications of these developments in data generation and manipulation. However, it is worth finishing this chapter by noting the impact that the massive rise in the reliance of businesses of data is having. At the micro level it is creating new occupations as demand for skilled data handlers grows. Davis (2019) notes the emergence of 'data hunters' who are able to source difficult-to-find datasets for use in AI and machine learning (ML) projects. As data exploitation through AI and ML techniques can offer a firm a significant competitive advantage over its rivals, finding relevant data to feed into the programmes is becoming more important. Data hunters are needed to track down relevant data from external sources such as public bodies and data marketplaces. At the macro level, governments are devising data policies to provide economic environments to encourage innovation amongst private firms. In 2019 the UK government announced a consultation to shape a National Data Strategy and improve the country's economic prospects for industrial growth based on the smarter use of data. While public projects to drive innovation often miss the mark as technology moves at a rate and in directions which could not be predicted, it is apparent that governments recognise the significance of the changes in the data landscape over the previous 20 years. The next chapter looks at these changes in more detail and considers the data strategies of the companies which have most successfully ridden this wave of innovation.

18 Origins of business data

References

Black, A. (2006). Information History. *ARIST*, *40*(1), 441–473.

Chandler, A.D. & Cortada, J.W. (2000). *A Nation Transformed by Information: How Information has Shaped the United States from Colonial Times to the Present*. Oxford University Press.

Chang, K. (2019, May 23). SpaceX Launches 60 Starlink Internet Satellites Into Orbit. *The New York Times*. www.nytimes.com/2019/05/23/science/spacex-launch.html.

Davis, J. (2019, May 13). Data Hunter: The New Sexy Technology Job. InformationWeek. www.informationweek.com/big-data/ai-machine-learning/data-hunter-the-new-sexy-technology-job/d/d-id/1334664.

Desjardins, J. (2017, August 29). The History of Consumer Credit in One Giant Infographic. Visual Capitalist. www.visualcapitalist.com/history-consumer-credit-one-infographic/.

Donnan, C. (2011). *A Brief History of Market Data*. European Financial Information Summit, London.

eMarketer (2018, March 28). US TV Ad Spending to Fall in 2018. www.emarketer.com/content/us-tv-ad-spending-to-fall-in-2018.

Graham, M. (2000). The Threshold of the Information Age. In *A Nation Transformed by Information: How Information has Shaped the United States from Colonial Times to the Present*, eds Chandler, A.D. and Cortada, J.W. Oxford University Press.

Harford, T. (2017, June 12). How the World's First Accountants Counted on Cuneiform. BBC News. www.bbc.com/news/business-39870485.

Lewis, M. (2015). *Flash Boys* (1st edn). Penguin.

Lockley, L.C. (1950). Notes on the History of Marketing Research. *Journal of Marketing*, *14*(5), 733–736.

Lyman, P. & Varian, H. (2000). How Much Information? University of California at Berkeley. http://groups.ischool.berkeley.edu/archive/how-much-info/.

Lyman, P. & Varian, H. (2003). How much information? University of California at Berkeley. http://groups.ischool.berkeley.edu/archive/how-much-info-2003/

Machlup, F. (1962). *The Production and Distribution of Knowledge in the United States*. Princeton University Press.

Meeker, M. (2019, June 11). *Internet Trends 2019*. Code 2019.

Ofcom (2018). *Communications Market Report*.

Porat, M.U. (1977). *The Information Economy: Definition and Measurement* (p. 242). Office of Telecommunications. https://eric.ed.gov/?id=ED142205.

Rayward, W.B. (2014). Information Revolutions, the Information Society, and the Future of the History of Information Science. *Library Trends*, *62*(3), 681–713.

Reinsel, D., Gantz, J. & Rydning, J. (2018). *The Digitization of the World: From Edge to Core*. IDC.

Reuters (2008, February 19). Reuters, from Pigeons to Multimedia Merger. www.reuters.com/article/us-reuters-thomson-chronology-idUSL1849100620080219.

Sears (2012). History of the Sears Catalog. www.searsarchives.com/catalogs/history.htm.

Shapiro, R. & Aneja, S. (2019). *Who Owns Americans' Personal Information and What Is It Worth?* Future Majority.

Smith, A. (1986). *The Wealth of Nations*. Penguin Books.

Standage, T. (1999). *The Victorian Internet* (new edn). W&N.

Taylor, F.W. (1911). *The Principles of Scientific Management*. Harper and Bros.

The Economist (2017, May 6). The World's Most Valuable Resource is No Longer Oil, but Data. www.economist.com/news/leaders/21721656-data-economy-demands-new-approach-antitrust-rules-worlds-most-valuable-resource.

Thirani, V. & Gupta, A. (2017, September 22). The Value of Data. World Economic Forum. www.weforum.org/agenda/2017/09/the-value-of-data/.

Watson, Healy, L. (2017). *Information Industry Outlook 2018* (p. 60). OutSell Inc.

Watson, N. (2013). A Brief History of Experian. Experian. www.experianplc.com/media/1323/8151-exp-experian-history-book_abridged_final.pdf.

Wilson, T.D. (2002). The Nonsense of Knowledge Management. *Information Research, 8*(1). www.informationr.net/ir/8-1/paper144.html.

Wu, T. (2016). *The Attention Merchants: The Epic Scramble to Get Inside Our Heads* (1st edn). Knopf.

Wylie, I., Nevitt, C., Carnie, K. & Barrett, H. (2013, February 18). How Business Data has Evolved. *Financial Times*. www.ft.com/content/5f130ed6-777a-11e2-9ebc-00144feabdc0.

Zweig, J. (2014, July 7). Wall Street, 1889: The Telegraph Ramps Up Trading Speed. *The Wall Street Journal*. www.wsj.com/articles/wall-street-1889-the-telegraph-ramps-up-trading-speed-1404765917.

3

DATA GENERATION AND USE IN THE TWENTY-FIRST CENTURY

The rise of the new data monopolies

The origins of the internet and the World Wide Web

The global data business we are seeing emerge today owes much to the rise of computing in the late twentieth century but equally to the networking of these new devices, which allowed them to be used in ways not imagined by technologists 30 years ago. The success of the internet as a global platform from which data relentlessly springs forth marked a move from closed, proprietary systems of computing and communications to a far more open network not owned by any single entity or beholden to proprietary standards. It is useful to understand the history and principles of the internet's architecture to appreciate how it has led to its position as the unrivalled source of innovation and data creation.

The internet is the result of technological innovation at the networking level, visionary computer scientists and political pressure at a national level in the US. The first documented discussions of a computer-based system that would allow social interactions can be traced back to 1962 when J.C.R. Licklider of the Massachusetts Institute of Technology (MIT) set out his vison for a 'Galactic Network' (Leiner et al., 2009). In his mind, the system would comprise a global network of computers where users would be able to access information from any of the nodes on the network. When Licklider moved to military research centre the Defense Advanced Research Projects Agency (DARPA) late in 1962 he took this idea with him and set the wheels in motion for his vision to become a reality.

At the same time as Licklider was refining his notion of a Galactic Network, other researchers were developing new and more efficient ways to transport data across networks using packet switching. Rather than moving data from one point to another on a network via a direct connection, packet switching broke messages into packets that could be directed across different routes within a network and reassembled at the receiving end. This more flexible arrangement provided

22 Data generation and use in the 21st century

redundancy into the system whereby if one part of the network went down the lost packets could be resent. This technology was adopted by DARPA in its ARPANET system, which went live in 1969. In the 1970s, the adoption of the TCP/IP protocol for exchanging data across the ARPANET resulted in the foundations for the internet as we know it today. Throughout the 1980s the ARPANET grew in reach as government research bodies and universities around the world joined the network and used it to communicate and share information.

One of these research organisations was the European Organization for Nuclear Research (CERN), where one of the computer scientists, Tim Berners-Lee, was growing frustrated at the inefficiencies of retrieving information across multiple computers. Inspired by work done in the 1960s and 1970s on hypertext as a way of linking concepts across electronic documents stored on multiple computers, Berners-Lee invented the World Wide Web (WWW) in 1989 and built the first web browser in 1990. Using the internet as the network on which to layer the WWW, the Web emerged as a mechanism for the presentation and linking of rich media files that were more user-friendly to a non-technical audience than the earlier file sharing systems.

The WWW grew rapidly in popularity as an internet application from ten websites in 1992 to 130 in 1993 and 2,738 in 1994 (Internet Live Stats, 2019). Users quickly found novel ways to share information using the WWW. In 1991, researchers at the University of Cambridge were frustrated that the coffee pot they shared in a staff room was often empty when they got there. To allow the researchers to check if the pot was empty before leaving their desks, several of them set up what was possibly the first webcam next to the machine, allowing them to view it live through their web browser.

It was the flexibility of the internet and the WWW that encouraged experiments such as the coffee cam. The standards and protocols underpinning them were open and freely available for anyone to tinker with and build applications. This contrasts with the other networks available at the time, such as CompuServe and AOL, which offered online information and communication services similar to the WWW and internet but were proprietary and operated by private entities for commercial gain. As Jonathan Zittrain, Professor of Internet Law at Harvard Law School and author of *The Future of the Internet*, describes the massive investments in their services made by these commercial organisations:

> All those bets lost. The proprietary networks went extinct, despite having accumulated millions of subscribers. They were crushed by a network built by government researchers and computer scientists who had no CEO, no master business plan, no paying subscribers, no investment in content, and no financial interest in accumulating subscribers.
>
> *(Zittrain, 2008, p. 7)*

Innovators rely on enabling technologies upon which to build their products and services and the more open and accessible these technologies are, the more likely they are to be utilised. Henry Ford did not invent the internal combustion engine but was able to use it because no permission or licensing arrangement was needed for him to adapt it for use in mass-produced cars. It is often those experimenting with new technologies at the edges that build the foundations for new waves of innovation. Berners-Lee and the WWW are a case in point.

By 1994 it was becoming clear to many observers of this emerging technology that the internet was going to be the technological platform from which a new information revolution could be built. During the early 1990s there was much talk of Information Superhighways that were going to revolutionise how we worked and lived but most commentators believed these networks would be the proprietary ones being built by telecommunications firms and cable operators such as AT&T and Time Warner. In many ways this was a natural conclusion as these companies had the expertise, financial resources, existing networks and customer bases from which to build the Information Superhighways. However, these companies were beginning to realise that the innovation and investments were starting to coalesce around the internet – and not their shiny, well-managed networks. The building blocks were in place by 1994 for several decades of data-driven innovation to begin and the rise of companies not yet founded to dominate key areas of our work and social lives.

Internet innovation wave 1: 1994–2000

In April 1994, *The New York Times* reported that a realistic number for global internet users was probably around the 3 million mark (Lewis, 1994). Others were estimating figures of up to 30 million, but whether it was 3 or 30 million, the proportion of the world's population using the internet was very small, perhaps 0.5% percent, compared to more than 60% in 2019. However, the rapid growth in users was what caught writers' and financiers' imaginations. It was becoming very clear that something was going on with this network that had the potential to change how people communicated and shared information. While academic and government research institutions had been the primary users for 20 years, consumers and businesses were now connecting to the network for email and to, according to the newly invented term, 'surf the Web'. As with any new form of media, investors were quick to investigate whether there were any opportunities to make money for these new activities. In late 1995, the investment bank Morgan Stanley published the first of several 'Internet Reports' for the company's clients to explore where the investment opportunities lay. It is interesting that the 322-page report devoted a large section to explaining what the internet was in terms of how it worked and how it could be accessed. Also interesting, from an historical perspective, are the three core areas of investment opportunities the two authors of the report identified. These were infrastructure, software and content. The main areas they focused on were infrastructure and software, as the backbone of a commercial internet was in its early stages and required massive investments to build out. Content as a category of companies for investment was a thinner section, reflecting the uncertainty over how

24 Data generation and use in the 21st century

businesses could turn a profit on their web content. AOL was emerging as a content platform for the internet but a lot of the discussion was on ways that established newspaper and magazine publishers might sell their content over the internet. With hindsight we can see how trying to predict the future of any rapidly evolving technology is almost impossible, and the internet was no exception. Twenty-five years later, the main winners of this revolution have been the content aggregators, such as Google, Facebook and Amazon, as the internet upended the business models of traditional information providers as the world moved from an era of data scarcity to one of abundance.

In the mid-1990s, two of the hottest properties on the Web were Yahoo! and Netscape. Yahoo! was founded in 1994 by Stanford students Jerry Yang and David Filo, who built a subject-based catalogue for finding websites. At the time, there were fewer than 3,000 websites globally and so the work required to do this was not extensive. Sites were organised according to the content they carried and users of Yahoo! could drill down into the catalogue until they found something appropriate. Revenue came from display advertising carried on the site's pages and by 1996 when the company went public, Yahoo! was valued at $848 million; four years later, at its peak, it was worth $125 billion (Johnson, 2016).

Netscape, also founded in 1994, was the first commercial web browser, created by Marc Andreessen and Jim Clark based on Andreessen's work with others at the University of Illinois in building the Mosaic browser. While the Netscape name may no longer be known by most web users, in the mid-1990s it represented for many the future of the Web. The WWW needed an easy-to-install and easy-to-use browser that non-technical PC owners could find their way around without a user manual. Netscape provided this and, even though in its early days users had to pay for it, by 1995 it was the most popular browser by far with an almost 80% market share. A flotation in August 1995 saw the share price double in its first day of trading, valuing the company at almost $3 billion (Planes, 2013). It is often claimed that the Netscape share offering kick-started the internet boom of the late 1990s as investors saw, for the first time, that a new and rapidly growing area of technology was emerging.

The central proposition to consumers of these two companies was the retrieval and presentation of data. Yahoo! helped web users find the information they needed from the universe of websites, while Netscape provided a gateway to the WWW and the riches it contained. The internet and the WWW resembled the Wild West, with few rules beyond websites having to conform to basic technical protocols, and no central point of control. The old media and communication model of centrally managed systems where content was chosen and presented by the network owners had radically changed and anyone with some technical knowledge could take part. This was an opportunity for content creators and entrepreneurs but a challenge for users who had to navigate this new world. As already mentioned, consumers were migrating from a world of information scarcity to one of abundance. For decades the media and information industries had been constrained by the limitations of the physical world. A country could only support so many newspapers and each newspaper could only contain so many pages. The broadcast radio and television networks were limited by the finite resource of the wireless spectrum. As a consequence, media was rationed and advertisers had little choice in where to place their money. Suddenly the rules had changed and a new order of unlimited websites with unlimited pages of content became possible. Entrepreneurs rushed in to stake their claims in this new frontier and investors followed, chasing new opportunities and anticipated rich returns.

However, misunderstandings about what a sustainable and profitable internet business might look like and unrealistic expectations of the capabilities of this nascent technology brought things to a shuddering halt in early 2000 when the so-called dotcom crash began. As start-ups raised funds at ever-increasing valuations based on little more than hope and then burned through their cash with little sign of significant revenues and less sign of profits, the realisation began to dawn that this could not continue. Between March 2000 and October 2002 the Nasdaq stock exchange in New York, where many dotcom companies listed their shares, fell by 78% (Alden, 2005). Many commentators concluded that the internet was just a fad and that the retail and media sectors would return to their traditional ways of doing business. As the next chapter shows, and as we all know, this was clearly wrong and simply marked the ending of one stage of innovation deployment and the beginning of another.

Internet innovation wave 2: 2000–2007

In her book *Technological Revolutions and Financial Capital*, economist and innovation scholar Carlota Perez makes the point that technological revolutions occur in stages that can be broadly divided into two key periods (Perez, 2003). These are the installation phase, where a new technology enters the market and investments are made in the required underpinning infrastructure, followed by the deployment phase, where members of society begin to adopt this new technology and innovations occur around its take-up. However, another feature of these revolutions is a financial crash followed by a recovery that occurs between the two stages. Examples of this can be seen with the canal and railway building in the UK in the eighteenth and nineteenth centuries. Massive speculative investments were made in these new transportation networks by private investors who saw the potential that the faster and cheaper transport of goods and people would bring to the emerging industrial economy. However, the returns on these investments took longer than many had thought, with many of the newly formed canal and railway companies going into administration. It could be argued that a similar way of thinking occurred in the late 1990s and the dotcom mania that ensued.

By early 2000 it was clear that the valuations of many internet-based companies had far exceeded their potential for profits and, as a result, the stampede of investors into the market had been followed by a rush for the exits. However, if we see the period from 1994 to 2000 as the 'installation' phase of the Internet Revolution, we should also view the subsequent seven years as the 'deployment' stage. While

26 Data generation and use in the 21st century

many companies either disappeared or were bought on the cheap and absorbed by industry incumbents, some such as eBay and Amazon continued to expand and draw in new customers. At the same time, new firms emerged to build products on the Web that grew organically by providing services people actually wanted to use and leveraging the unique capabilities of the internet to share data almost frictionlessly. Myspace, YouTube, Tumblr and later Facebook demonstrated the potential of the internet to facilitate networks for communication, entertainment and information sharing in a way that was not possible on the telecommunication networks of the previous century. The phrase 'Web 2.0' was coined to describe this new breed of companies that utilised technologies developed in the 'installation' phase to create more immersive and interactive websites than the more static sites from before the crash.

Supporting these developments was the mass deployment of broadband networks across most developed economies and the falling price of computing devices. As PCs and faster internet connections entered more homes and workplaces, new services such as video streaming and music downloading became possible. At the same time mobile networks were being upgraded to 3G, extending the internet to people on the move. In 2000, five mobile operators spent £22.47 billion on 3G licences from the UK government, with similarly high bidding for 3G spectrum across other European countries (BBC News, 2000). It was still not clear how money could be made from the Web 2.0 era but public and commercial thirst for faster data connections was obvious and, it was hoped, new business models would emerge to justify these investments. Two developments from this period pointed the way to a profitable future: Google AdWords and the Apple iPhone.

At the end of 1999, Google employed only 39 people, most of them engineers, and needed to find a way to earn money from its popular and successful search engine. The company was handling more than 5 million search queries a day, which grew to 18 million by mid-2000. As stated by John Battelle, author of *The Search*, which chronicles Google's early history:

> With more than $500,000 (and growing) going out the door each month and less than $20 million in the bank, you didn't need a Stanford PhD to do the math: the company needed a business model that worked.
>
> *(Battelle, 2006, p. 123)*

In 2000, the company launched its AdWords service, which allowed advertisers to place small, text-based ads alongside search results. There was a clear delineation between Google's 'natural' or 'organic' search results and the ads so that users were not confused. The service was successful and during 2001 Google earned more than $80 million from it. Advertisers paid Google on the basis of how many people saw their ads (CPM), a model that newspapers and television had followed for decades. However, in 2002 the company changed this approach and moved to an auction and pay-per-click model. Advertisers would now set a maximum for how much they were prepared to pay when someone clicked on their ad rather than using a simple CPM basis. To prevent companies from simply paying their way to the top, Google incorporated a popularity variable into the ranking algorithm based on how many people had already clicked on the ad. This meant that relevance to users was part of the ranking for ads, similar to the organic results. The impact was immediate, with total revenues of $440 million in 2002, rising to $3 billion by the end of 2004.

While vital to the future of Google as a company, the success of the AdWords service is more important for what it tells us about the value of data. In some ways, AdWords is not doing anything differently to what media companies in the publishing and television sectors have done for nearly 100 years. Google is selling the attention or 'eyeballs' of its audience to companies that want to sell them their products and services. However, the crucial difference is that extra bit of data which Google sells and then the ability of the internet to immediately take someone to a specific web page. The extra bit of data is the word or phrase that someone typed in to the Google search box. That, as Battelle (2006) describes it, allows Google to build its 'Database of Intentions', which can match what someone wants with what a company is offering. Such precision in targeting was unique to the marketing sector and provided a cost-effective way for advertisers to reach their potential customers. Gone was the wastage seen in traditional advertising channels where mass audiences were paid in the hope that some of those seeing the ad would respond positively to it. This old way of doing things is best summarised in the quote often attributed to successful American department store owner John Wanamaker, who is reputed to have said, 'Half the money I spend on advertising is wasted; the trouble is, I don't know which half'. By matching allowing advertisers to bid for keywords in search terms and then only charging them when someone clicks on their ad, the mismatch between targeting and interaction is broken. On top of this, when an ad is clicked on the searcher is taken directly to the relevant web page of the advertiser, rather than, as with traditional media, hoping the consumer will take some action in the future. This simple change saw Google's (now called Alphabet Inc.) revenues climb to almost $140 billion in 2018, with more than 80% of this coming from the company's advertising services.

While Google demonstrated how a new data-driven advertising model could work on the internet, it took Apple to show how mobile devices could provide the next stage in the evolution of computing and communications. Mobile phones were first launched in the mid-1980s and by the early 2000s had become mass consumer devices through the combination of cheaper handsets and pay-as-you-go tariffs. So-called smartphones had been launched by various manufacturers from the late 1990s and Microsoft had released its mobile operating system, Windows CE, in 1996. However, none of these devices were successful due to a combination of high prices and poor user interfaces. This changed in 2007 when Apple launched the iPhone. Although the first model did not have 3G capabilities and there was no app store, its buttonless, touch-screen interface was popular with users and has remained the dominant design for phones since then. The following year Apple released its app store and Google launched its first Android phone. With these

28 Data generation and use in the 21st century

innovations the next phase of the information revolution had begun and the central role of data-driven innovation was established.

Internet innovation wave 3: 2007–2018

During this third wave of innovation, data came to the fore as a driver of new services and, as a result, new business models. Smartphones played an important part in this transformation as computers could now be carried with users wherever they went. Mobile broadband networks and WiFi allowed almost ubiquitous connectivity and the ability of phones to know their exact location though GPS, as well as take photos, provided a platform for services such as Google Maps, Instagram and localised search results. This in turn provided more opportunities for advertisers to target users against location as well as just search terms.

The explosion in smartphone ownership from 2007 reinvigorated a maturing technology sector. Annual global sales of smartphones rose from 122 million in 2007 to more than 1.5 billion in 2018 (Statista, 2019c). While more than three-quarters of adults in most developed economies owned a smartphone by 2018, the revolution also spread to emerging nations. Poorer countries that had largely missed the first telecommunications revolution of the twentieth century leapfrogged the age of wired networks and went straight to wireless. The result has been a dynamic ecosystem of manufacturers, wireless carriers and app developers which have built thriving ecommerce and communication platforms. Google and Apple dominate the smartphone operating system sector, with Android taking 75% and iOS 23% by early 2019 (Casserly, 2019).

Relying on these two operating systems are the millions of apps used by smartphone owners and it is the data shared across these services which has fuelled this third wave of innovation. Industry consultants Deloitte (2017) estimate that individuals on average hold data relationships with around 35 app operators across a range of sectors and activities including ecommerce, gaming, gambling, social media, travel, financial and media. The utility that smartphones and their apps offer has encouraged data sharing by consumers in return for the value received as a result. Some of the fastest-growing companies of this third wave are built on data-driven business models where the smartphone is typically the data source. Uber, Deliveroo, Just Eat, Instagram, Snapchat, Pinterest and Airbnb have constructed their offerings around mobile devices and the value of the data their services generate.

However, the value of these new streams of data goes beyond just the advertising industry and the opportunities for more precise targeting. Behind the scenes, the value of data to transform other sectors and business activities was realised in this third wave. As computing devices and applications were applied within a range of industrial settings, it became apparent that data could be applied as a disruptive force across the entire economy. The rise of the Internet of Things (IoT), machine learning (ML) and artificial intelligence (AI) provided a glimpse into a future where data-driven decision making could transform how we work and live. Broadly this can be divided into three areas of activity: in the workplace, in the home and on

Data generation and use in the 21st century **29**

our bodies. The final chapter will explore in more detail these areas of technology in terms of where they may be taking us, but at this stage it is important to understand their evolution in terms of the data landscape.

Although computers have been used within the business sector since the 1950s, their impact has largely been the digitisation of back-office functions such as payroll, logistics and customer relationship management. Industrial firms such as car makers have been using 'robots' on the assembly line since the 1970s but the systems supporting production were still largely designed and run by humans. During this third wave of innovation, the notion of 'smart manufacturing', sometimes referred to as 'Industry 4.0', emerged to describe the application of AI, ML and the IoT to established working practices and environments. In this emerging model, entire supply chains as well as the manufacturing processes themselves are managed by software that is driven by real-time data. The data is generated through the embedding of sensors and communication devices which can track activities and the movement of goods through the system from suppliers of raw materials through to the final delivery stage. The efficiencies such systems facilitate would ripple through the supply chain, saving trillions of dollars and raising the competitive bar for companies not part of such a system. Germany, a country heavily reliant on its manufacturing base, has recognised the threat such smart manufacturing techniques pose to its companies and, during this period, has invested in developing its own 'Industrie 4.0' strategy. As the country's chancellor Angela Merkel stated in 2015:

> We need to quickly master the amalgamation of the world of the internet with the world of industrial production because the current leaders in the digital area will otherwise take over industrial production.
>
> *(Schroeder, 2016, p. 1)*

Just as industry is incorporating data-driven technologies into its factories and offices, so too are domestic households. Smart devices such as the Amazon Echo, Google Home and associated smart doorbells, lighting and heating systems emerged during this third wave to a generally warm reception by consumers. While many were concerned about possible losses of privacy through devices that were always listening for commands, many more were happy to allow Google, Amazon and Apple into their homes. In the UK in 2019 a quarter of households (6.8 million) had installed one of these devices and this was expected to rise to 44% by 2023 (Statista, 2019b). As a source of data for measuring household occupier activity, smart devices have an obvious value as they provide a platform, similar to the smartphone, from which to launch further applications and services.

Finally, our bodies are becoming places for data gathering technologies via smart watches, activity monitors and fitness trackers. In many ways, these have the potential to transform our lives in more significant ways than the smartphone, Industry 4.0 and smart home devices. Health data is perhaps the most valuable – both to us in terms of our wellbeing but also to healthcare providers, insurers and the pharmaceutical industry. A smartphone can tell companies where we are and who we are

30 Data generation and use in the 21st century

communicating with. An Amazon Echo or Google Home may be able to sense who is in the room and what they want to do. However, a smart watch or fitness tracker is able to monitor vital signs such as heart rate, activity levels, blood sugar readings and, with some newer devices, blood pressure. These can provide early warning signs of health problems but also, over time, can build up a picture of the current and potential future health of its owner. For health insurers this can be used to calculate more accurate premiums based on the policy holder's lifestyle and we will look at the privacy implications of this in Chapter 4. Organisations, public and private, engaged in medical research are also keen to access this information as large-scale, time-series lifestyle and vital-sign datasets are expensive to create. With 22% (57 million) of the US population wearing some kind of smart device in 2019, the potential for unprecedented volumes of accurate health data to be collected and used to better understand the relationship between disease and lifestyle choices has never been greater.

The monetisation of the Web

When Tim Berners-Lee created the WWW in 1989 he did not do so for personal profit but rather to build a technology that would make information retrieval and sharing easier. He saw the WWW as a:

> vision encompassing the decentralised, organic growth of ideas, technology, and society. The vision I have for the Web is about anything being potentially connected with anything.
>
> *(Berners-Lee and Fischetti, 1999, p. 1)*

While his vision for a decentralised system for sharing ideas has taken shape, little did he realise what a data-generating, money-making machine it would also be. Trillions of dollars of value have been created from his idea, particularly within the marketing industry. This section considers how this data flows through the Web, where the money is being made and by whom.

Google, followed by Facebook, is the leader in the $200-billion ad technology industry, with a market share approaching two-thirds of all digital advertising expenditure in 2019. Below it sits a dynamic mixture of technology companies and agencies that offer services and products to help marketers spend their advertising budgets and reach consumers. At the heart of all this activity is the collection and analysis of data on the search, surfing and social media habits of billions of people. Providing fluidity to this market for personal data are the data brokers that slice, dice and combine data from multiple sources to build up rich pictures of target customer groups and sell these audiences on to advertisers. The ethics and legality of some of these activities are considered in Chapter 4, but before those issues can be understood it is important to know how the industry operates.

Before the rise of the Web, placing advertisements so they would be seen by a target audience was a relatively straightforward business. An advertiser would decide on a budget for a marketing campaign to support a particular product or service and, typically, an advertising agency would be appointed to produce the creative work and then buy space in the media to place it. Media planners and buyers worked within agencies to decide which media would be most appropriate to reach the intended audience and then negotiate with media owners such as newspapers, magazines and television channels to buy space. Third-party auditing organisations then conducted surveys to estimate how many people had seen the advertising based on television viewership figures and newspaper and magazine sales. For most of the twentieth century this arrangement worked to the mutual benefit of advertisers and media owners, with agencies generally taking a percentage of the media spend. However, as mentioned in an earlier section, building up a real and accurate understanding of how effective the advertising had been in terms of changing consumer behaviour and driving sales was more of an art than a science. The Web has changed that, with a back-channel in the form of the internet feeding data directly back to marketers in terms of clicks and the time spent on web pages. Rather than 'guessing' how many people had seen your advertisement and then trying to calculate if an increase in sales of your breakfast cereal was as a result of this, advertisers can now access real-time information on the impact of their marketing spend.

In the early days of the Web, advertising was generally confined to banner advertisements placed around Web pages. Advertisers tended to pay on the basis of how many people had seen their ads (CPM), which could be calculated relatively accurately based on analytics software monitoring website activity. Advertisers could also tell how many people had clicked on the ads and been taken to their own sites by running the same software themselves. As we saw previously, Google introduced a new layer of targeting into the mix by allowing advertisers to bid for specific keywords typed into the search engine. This added far greater accuracy in terms of targeting relevant audiences but also made budgets go further on the basis of advertisers only paying when a user clicked on their ad.

More recently, new techniques have been introduced to automate the process of Web advertising using the large amounts of data on consumer behaviour which have been compiled by agencies through consumers use of the internet. This is often referred to as programmatic advertising and, much in the same way that most stock market trading is carried out by computers, removes the need for people to make many of the media buying decisions. It typically involves two systems talking to each other to agree on where ads should be placed and how much should be paid. Website owners with advertising space or inventory to sell use a supply-side platform (SSP) which has details of what space is for sale, the price and the audiences being offered on those sites. Advertisers use a demand-side platform (DSP) to outline their budget, impressions required and target audience. The two platforms then share this information to find matches. At the core of the process is the use of data to find better matches between advertiser needs and the what media owners have to offer in terms of audiences.

Under the broad banner of programmatic advertising sits real-time bidding (RTB). RTB allows more personalised targeting of individual web users based on their online behaviour. The real-time element refers to the ability of advertisers to

32 Data generation and use in the 21st century

bid to have their ad placed in front of a specific user via automated bidding, which takes milliseconds. This practice has become controversial due to the large amounts of personal data being used in the bidding process. The data presented to advertisers typically includes a user's location, IP address, time zone, type of device, browser type, previous search queries made on the current site and click behaviour. It may also include data from third-party cookies which track user behaviour across multiple sites. By using all this data, a rich picture can be built up of a single user and relevant ads placed in front of them via the real-time bidding system. RTB explains why an ad for a product a Web user was looking at on one site suddenly appears on a different site; that data was carried over from one site to another via a third-party cookie. For advertisers this makes for more effective targeting and for content owners it extends their potential audience.

In is estimated that 68% of all money spent on digital media advertising in 2020 will be programmatically traded, amounting to $98 billion (Zenith, 2018). While much of this will go to the media owners that create the content, there is also a thriving system of technology companies running the ad exchanges at both the demand and supply side. These firms are pure data companies in that they only exist to collect, process and share data in a market which did not exist 15 years ago. They have found ways to monetise the clicks and searches which billions of consumers engage in on a daily basis. However, they are minnows compared to the giants of the internet, which have built the data-driven empires discussed in the following sections. Understanding how these companies have used data to create value helps us understand some of the key business models driving innovation and provides a context to consider the next phase of a more decentralised Web.

The Google story

Google's ad business was explained in a previous section but it is worth exploring the other aspects to its business model and how the collection of data is central to the company's DNA. Although the Google business was renamed Alphabet Inc. in 2015, with the Google search business becoming a subsidiary, this book will continue to refer to the company as Google for the sake of simplicity.

Google was founded in 1998 by PhD students Sergey Brin and Larry Page. Its origins can be traced back to 1996 when Brin and Page were working on their PhDs at Stanford University and were looking to create an algorithm to better rank Web search results. Most search engines at the time simply measured how many times the search term appeared on a page as well as looking at the metadata of the page. Web pages where the search term appeared most were ranked more highly than other pages. A problem for users of these search engines was that the ranking did not take into account any measure of quality. Website owners quickly realised that stuffing their pages with specific keywords would raise their ranking and, as a result, their exposure. This could be profitably monetised by carrying advertising on those pages. Brin and Page's approach was to devise an algorithm they called PageRank, which introduced an element of quality into the ranking. They did this by analysing the links going into a page from other Web pages and inferred that pages with a higher number of inbound links were of higher quality and relevance due to their popularity. The algorithm also took into account the quality of the links themselves by measuring how many links were going into the referring pages. Compared to results from competitors such as Lycos and AltaVista, Google's search results were of far greater relevance to users and the company's search engine when launched in 1998 quickly became the most popular. In 2004 the company became public by issuing shares on the Nasdaq stock exchange and between the flotation in August 2004 and April 2019 the shares rose in price from $54 to $1,277, reflecting the value of the company, which generated profits of almost $31 billion on $137 billion of revenue in 2018 (Alphabet, 2019).

While more than three-quarters of the company's revenue is generated through its advertising services, it is useful to examine the other parts of the business to see how they contribute to the world's largest advertising platform. Google's publicly stated mission is 'to organise the world's information and make it universally access-ible and useful' (Google, 2019). The company and its diverse operations should be seen within that context as it continues to drive its core activities and investments. Underpinning this mission is the unwritten corporate strategy of monetising this information by placing advertising around and within it.

The mission to make information more accessible to internet users explains initiatives such as Google Books, Google News and Google Scholar. All these ser-vices have utilised the company's expertise in indexing large quantities of data and repackaging it in more user-friendly ways for consumers. But what about Google's Android mobile operating system, Google Maps and its move into selling smart home devices? These do not immediately seem to fit with crawling, indexing and presenting information from the Web. It is important to see these innovations as Google's attempt to be relevant in a world where the PC is no longer the main device for searching the Web, as well as extending its reach to other activities that offer potential for targeted advertising.

Google bought Android Inc. in 2005 when it realised that mobile computing devices, now commonly referred to as smartphones, could become a viable alter-native to the less portable PC. Google had cemented its position as the dominant search engine for Web users by this time, but it was not clear that Web search would be so popular on mobile devices. The company feared that phone makers and developers of mobile operating systems might find their own ways to offer a search service, bypassing Google altogether. The launch of Apple's iPhone in 2007 and the realisation that a viable, portable alternative to the PC had emerged focused the company's efforts in this space and the first Android phones were released in 2008. Unlike Apple's proprietary mobile operating system and its policy of not allowing other companies to make phones that could run iOS, Google adopted a more open approach. Its core business is not in making hardware but in managing informa-tion and so the company allowed manufacturers to put Android on their phones as a way of rapidly achieving market share. From Google's perspective, the more Android phones there were, the more opportunities there were to control mobile searching. While the Android operating system is open in that anyone can download and use it, Google does set some conditions for handset makers that want to use the Google app store, including giving priority to Google search. The strategy has worked well for the company with Android enjoying a 76% global market share of all smartphone operating systems against Apple's 22% share (Statcounter, 2019). The importance of Android to Google is highlighted by the $12 billion the company is estimated to have paid Apple in 2019 to make its search engine the default on Apple's iPhones (Segarra, 2018).

Other initiatives such as Google Maps and Google Home devices should be seen in a similar light to its Android strategy. Digital mapping services for smartphones offer significant opportunities for contextual advertising. Map users are often looking for local businesses such as shops and restaurants and Google's My Business service offers these small firms a way to achieve visibility on searches within Google Maps. Google Home products provide the company with a gateway to voice-activated smart devices and could be viewed as a hedge against a move by users to talk to their devices rather than type words into a screen. Placing advertising alongside the automated voice responses from a Google Home device is a challenge but the company would rather control the technology and figure this puzzle out later than let a new entrant colonise the space. This strategy worked well with Web search and the commercial radio sector shows how an advertising-driven, voice-based service can work.

The Facebook story

Facebook's 2004 origins in the Harvard dorm room of Mark Zuckerberg are well known. Initially created to allow Harvard students to rate the attractiveness of their classmates, the social network has long since been a global phenomenon, with an estimated 2.38 billion users in early 2019 (Statista, 2019a). The company also owns through acquisitions WhatsApp and Instagram. In the context of this book, the company is of particular interest through its business model based around the capture and then selling of data about the likes, connections and habits of its users. It is also interesting because it exemplifies the benefits for data-driven companies of being able to exploit network effects.

The concept of network effects has its origins in the field of economics and from this perspective is defined as the:

> utility that a user derives from consumption of goods ... [which] increases with the number of other agents consuming the [same] good.
>
> *(Katz and Shapiro, 1985, p. 424)*

In some ways this can be seen as the opposite to the traditional supply-and-demand model of economic value whereby the greater the scarcity of a commodity, the higher its value will generally be. Products or services subject to network effects – or network externalities, as they are also referred to – will be perceived as having higher value when there are more people consuming. This is particularly apparent in communication networks based around technologies such as the telephone or email. In the late nineteenth century when the telephone was still an expensive novelty, there was little incentive for consumers or businesses to have one installed as there were very few other telephone users to talk to. As the network slowly grew, it became more likely that potential subscribers would know of someone who already had a telephone and so had more of a reason to install one themselves. The same principle applied to email in the 1990s. Eventually there is a tipping point when most people are connected to the communications system and non-subscribers are put under increasing pressure to also join. From the perspective of the network operators, network effects offer the potential to attract new customers without having to solely rely on expensive marketing; the network markets itself. Facebook was no different and as the social network spread out from the Harvard campus, consumers began to hear friends and family members talk about this new way of sharing information and so were encouraged to join themselves. The speed of adoption was hastened by the ease and zero cost of signing up. Where the telephone took over 70 years for more than half of the US population to have one in the home, Facebook took less than ten.

Like Google, Facebook's business model is based around selling its audience to advertisers. However, it differs in the data that it uses to target advertising and this reflects the way in which it is generally more closely integrated into the lives of its user base. While Google relies largely on the words typed into its search engine to target ads, Facebook is able to draw on a richer pool of data. Depending on how honest people are when they sign up for an account, it will know a user's date of birth, gender, location, schools and colleges attended and other lifestyle information. It also knows who its users are connected to and the types of content users read, like and follow. Combining all this data with third-party data it pays for, Facebook is able to offer extremely precise targeting variables to its advertisers. This can be down to granular details such as occupation, level of education, average salary, relationship status and number of children, or even if the user is pregnant. By combing this level of detail with a user base of billions, the company offers the second-largest advertising platform with a revenue in 2018 of $55 billion (Facebook, 2019).

While there are signs that the rate of growth of the company is slowing and, amongst some age groups, even falling, Facebook has become an important part of billions of lives. It caters to a basic human need for connection and, because of network effects, it would be very difficult for a competitor to build a viable alternative. Its successful migration from the PC to a smartphone world has created the world's most successful data-gathering platform.

> You dedicate thirty-five minutes of each of your days to Facebook. Combined with its other properties, Instagram and WhatsApp, that number jumps to fifty minutes. People spend more time on the platform than any behaviour outside of family, work, or sleep.
>
> *(Galloway, 2018, p. 90)*

36 Data generation and use in the 21st century

However, as we shall see in a later section, there is a darker side to a single company controlling this much personal information. Although capturing data on the types of Facebook content that people like as well as other demographic information may seem innocuous on the surface, it can be used for opaque social manipulation that may not serve democracy. The ways in which political campaigners used Facebook's advertising platform to target ads at very specific groups of people in the 2016 US presidential election and the UK's EU referendum have illustrated how little data is required to identify voters that can be influenced by misleading messages. Combined with the transient nature of Facebook advertising and the lack of a public archive of posted ads, tracing these messages and finding out who saw them in the run-up to those votes has proven almost impossible. Chapter 4 explores these issues in more detail and outlines some of the regulatory approaches that are being considered.

The Amazon story

Although most people think of Amazon as a large and successful online retailer, it is actually a data-driven company that happens to operate an ecommerce business. Founded in 1992 by Jeff Bezos with $1 million in funding, the firm went public in 1997 with shares rising 118,000% in value by July 2019 to make it the most valuable company in the world, valued at $985 billion. The key ingredient behind the company's success has been its use of data to help customers make purchase decisions, predict the popularity of new products and deal with suppliers. Emerging from its large-scale operations, the company has also built a suite of digital services that power many of the most popular websites and apps of the twenty-first century. According to Bezos, the company is built on three pillars (CB Insights, 2019a):

1. Amazon Prime – the bundling of digital services with free deliveries for Prime members;
2. Amazon Web Services – digital infrastructure and cloud computing services for business customers;
3. Marketplace – ecommerce services and 'shelf space' for third-party sellers.

The company's core business of ecommerce is built on offering the widest selection of choices for products categories and the lowest prices. This goes back to Bezos's original strategy of constantly seeking growth through undercutting competitors on price and exceeding them on customer service. Higher volumes of sales allow lower margins and prices, which then result in ever-more sales. Behind this is a virtuous circle of data collection and use. As more customers use Amazon, the company collects more data about their preferences, which then feeds into better customer service and product selection, thus attracting more customers and helping to retain existing ones. As time goes on it becomes increasingly difficult for existing retailers and new entrants to compete on price or customer service. In some cases, the company has purchase data on its customers going back more than two decades.

This provides a unique capability to tailor what the Amazon 'experience' is for its users including what products to show on the home page and specific offers or suggestions to make for future purchases.

Amazon Prime supports this strategy by integrating the company more deeply into the lives of its customers through same-day and next-day as well as free delivery. Bundled music and video streaming services help cement this relationship as does the integration of devices such as Kindle ebook readers, Amazon Fire tablets and the Echo. Not only do these technologies help sell more Amazon services and, in the case of Prime, help subsidise a loss-making delivery service, they also provide another valuable source of data for the company.

The Amazon Marketplace helps the company extends its product offerings to customers but also provides valuable data for its own product portfolio. Acting as the market controller gives the company a bird's-eye view of what products from third-party sellers are popular, who is buying them and the prices being paid.

While automation of its warehouses and distribution depots has been a vital part of its success, the application of automated processes through AI to its traditionally white-collar functions is also taking place. The 20-plus years of data on customer preferences and seasonal fluctuations in sales it has built up are being analysed by the company's data scientists to automate the buying process. Amazon has discovered that, in many cases, its algorithms are able to make better choices about how much inventory to stock than its human buyers (Soper, 2018).

It is clear that Amazon has more valuable data and better skills at using that data than traditional, brick-and-mortar retailers. The empty shops on high streets around the world are partly due to that imbalance. It is also apparent that its online competitors in many countries are struggling to keep up and, apart from niche retailers, it is difficult to see that changing in the short to medium term. However, more surprising is the threat the company poses to other successful digital players. Amazon Music poses a real threat to the aspirations of Spotify and Apple Music, while Amazon Video is a meaningful rival to Netflix both in terms of subscribers and investments in original content. Even Google is not immune to the Amazon juggernaut. As entrepreneur and business school professor Scott Galloway puts it:

> Google is, relatively speaking, losing to Amazon. Amazon is Google's largest customer and is better at optimizing search than Google is at optimizing Amazon.
>
> *(Galloway, 2018, p. 57)*

Google's advertising revenue is heavily reliant on searches for specific branded products and as Amazon extends its customer base, consumers are increasingly starting their research on the Amazon site. Not only does this threaten the core business of Google; it also reduces Amazon's costs by removing the need to advertise on search engines. When Amazon is the starting point rather than just one of many potential destinations from a Google search, the company's virtuous circle of more customers leading to more data leading to more customers becomes even stronger.

38 Data generation and use in the 21st century

The Apple story

Apple is famous for its high-end, expensive hardware products, particularly the iPhone. Although it did not invent the smartphone, it created the first one with mass appeal. Between its launch in 2007 and the end of 2018, more than 2.2 billion iPhones were sold (Costello, 2019). Unlike Facebook, Google and Amazon, Apple does not have its origins in the internet but was formed two decades before, in the 1970s. It is, therefore, not a data-first company in that its core business model is selling hardware supported by an ecosystem of software and media content. However, the company is evolving to a more data-centric model as the value of its products and services will increasingly rely on the capture and manipulation of data generated through customer usage. This is becoming evident with its smart home devices, smart watches and content services.

In its more than 40-year history, Apple has learned important lessons about the linking of hardware with software services to create ecosystems which will lock customers in and drive future products sales. In the 1980s, this was an expensive lesson for the company as its Apple Mac computer range, although more popular with users, lost out to the IBM PC and subsequent PC clones. At the heart of this defeat was the closed nature of Apple's computer platform. Apple did not license other manufacturers to make computers running the Mac OS but followed a strategy of making both the hardware and the OS itself. In the short term, this resulted in significant profits for the firm but, as the more open PC platform encouraged third parties to make PCs and peripherals, its market share of this rapidly growing sector began to decline. By 1998 Apple's share of global personal computer sales had fallen to 2.5% compared to the PC's 97.5%, a halving of its market share from only two years previously (Reimer, 2005). It was the company's launch of the iPod in 2001 and the iTunes Store in 2003 that set it back onto a solid growth trajectory as a consumer electronics firm. The iTunes Store offered a legal and easy way for consumers to pay for and download music and its integration with the iPod formed the basis for a dynamic ecosystem of hardware, software and media content. A similar approach with the iPhone and App Store a few years later was even more successful for Apple and demonstrated how an integrated platform could better serve customers and drive product sales. The iTunes and App Stores helped Apple build direct relationships with its customers through the payment process where real names, physical addresses and credit card details could be combined with purchase histories and consumption habits. The value of this data in terms of helping the company better understand its users and improve the products and services it offered as a result created a virtuous circle similar to Amazon's.

Two more recent innovations from Apple are built on this principle of using data to provide richer services: Siri and the Apple Watch. Siri is the company's voice-powered virtual assistant that is embedded into Apple hardware including phones, iPads, computers and watches. Its value to users lies in the ability to ask Siri questions without having to use a keyboard. For Apple it widens the range of scenarios within which its products can be used and allows them to be more tightly integrated into customers' lives. It also provides the basis for much richer data on what its customers are doing, their interests and lifestyles. Like the data from iTunes and the App Store, it helps strengthen the relationship with consumers and makes it more difficult for them to move to competing products and platforms.

The Apple Watch is more interesting in that its focus on collecting health-related data offers the potential for it to be part of a data platform more important to users than its music or software services have been. By its nature, health data can be extremely valuable in monitoring for potentially fatal conditions and, as more data is gathered over time, it is of interest to medical research firms. The Apple Watch has the potential to become an even more important part of Apple's future than the iPhone. With global health spending of more than $7 trillion in 2019, a mass-market device that can collect a range of fundamental health data and share it with the medical research community could help transform the development of new drugs and procedures as well as be highly profitable for Apple (CB Insights, 2019b). Taking lessons from the success of its iTunes and App Stores and how they formed the basis of ecosystems that drew users in, Apple is adopting a similar approach with its smart watch. The company recognises that it cannot control this ecosystem on its own and needs to work with the medical and healthcare sectors to develop common standards for the sharing of patient data across systems. This strategy has seen Apple involved in promoting Fast Healthcare Interoperability Resources (FIHR) technology that describes data formats and elements as well as an API for the efficient exchange of health data. The iPhone health app that connects to the Apple Watch can read data that is structured within the FIHR framework and allows users to see their medical records from a variety of US hospitals. Among technology companies, Apple is not alone in offering consumer-facing digital health services that utilise FIHR but its unique position as a global leader in the provision of smart technology puts it in a strong position to lead the health data revolution.

Data strategy models

The analysis of the ways the four companies discussed above are using data to drive revenue growth presents a variety of approaches. Each in their own way has been enormously successful with their business models, creating many billions of dollars of value for their shareholders. However, they also each raise challenges from a commercial viewpoint but also, perhaps more importantly, from social and legal perspectives. At the beginning of the third decade of the twenty-first century, increasingly loud voices are being raised by regulators, policy groups and politicians about the need for action to challenge aspects of the companys' business models, particularly with respect to Google, Facebook and Amazon.

At the heart of these criticisms is a concern about the ecosystems that these companies have built which, it is argued, threaten consumer rights and effective competition in the marketplace. We have seen how network effects have helped the big four drive customer acquisition and revenue growth. A side-effect of network effects that benefits the company exploiting them but can be detrimental to the interests of

40 Data generation and use in the 21st century

consumers is customer lock-in. The very thing that attracts users to a platform also makes it difficult for them to leave once they have joined. Lock-in may be due to proprietary technical standards: the iOS operating system, for example. Or it may be because the application of network effects has rendered the competition unprofitable, thus reducing the options to users of viable alternatives. In much of the world consumers have a variety of choices in the types and makes of cars they can purchase or the types of washing powder to use. However, that choice does not really exist in terms of the social network they may wish to join. If they want to use a network that most of their friends and family are on then it probably has to be Facebook. Some might argue that Instagram is a possibility but then realise that Facebook bought the company in 2012. This highlights another issue with the 'winner-takes-all' impact of network effects. The wealth generated by these companies allows them to buy up smaller competitors if they feel threatened by them.

In terms of how the big four are using data to drive their profitability, we can see some distinct differences in approach. Google and Facebook's advertising-driven business model contrasts with Amazon's use of data to drive its ecommerce model and Apple using it to drive hardware sales. A problem with an advertising-driven approach in terms of drawing the attention of regulators is that it relies on sharing data with third parties: advertisers. To demonstrate the value that their advertising platforms offer, Google and Facebook have to exchange user data relating to socio-economic, lifestyle and online behaviour with the companies placing ads. Amazon's collection and use of customer data is primarily used for internal purposes related to increasing sales of its inventory while Apple has consciously adopted a privacy-focused approach to how it manages user data. In 2017, researchers at Oxford university analysed almost 1 million apps on the Google app store in terms of how they collect and use data. They found that nearly 90% of the apps were set up to share data with Google (Ram, 2018). As well as sharing with Google they also discovered that the median app could transfer data to 10 third parties while 20% of apps could share with more than 20. The data being collected and shared includes age, gender and location as well as information about every other app installed on the phone. To a lesser but still significant degree many of the apps were also sharing data with Amazon and Facebook. According to Joel Reardon, Assistant Professor of Computer Science at the University of Calgary, smartphones are unique in their ability to collect sensitive and valuable data.

> Mobile phone are stores of sensitive information and if your phone is on, they're just sending the information all the time to the same third parties. Even just the characterisation of what apps you have on your phone is quite an insight into a person's life, you can learn information about their age, sexual orientation, health and link it back to their device.
>
> *(Ram, 2018)*

Another side-effect of the data-driven advertising business models employed by Facebook and Google is their thirst for content to draw in users and place advertisements next to. In the media models of the twentieth century the media owners were the originators of content which they invested in through the work of journalists and entertainers to create distinct platforms which appealed to specific audiences. Some newspapers opted for a mass-appeal, tabloid format to deliver large audiences, while others invested in more upmarket broadsheet papers for smaller but more lucrative readers. Magazines were even more niche in the markets they targeted, while television channels produced a variety of programming that spanned genres and the tastes of viewers. These expensive and time-consuming models contrast with those of Google and Facebook, which do not produce any of their own content but rely on the posts of users or third-party content crawled from the Web. This is obviously a much less expensive operation to manage but it comes often at the expense of traditional media. In a world where Google and Facebook are the primary gateways through which billions of people find and consume information, the value shifts from those creating the content to those managing the gates. In 2014, sales of two popular UK newspapers, the *Sun* and *The Guardian*, fell by 10% in just one year (Jackson, 2015). Regional newspapers have also been impacted by the rise of the Web, with many closing down or becoming online-only. In the UK between 2012 and 2018, advertising expenditure across all traditional media formats fell while media spend on online advertising more than doubled to over £13 billion (Ofcom, 2019). Newspapers and magazines were the biggest losers in this shift and, as a result, a number of enquiries have been launched into their commercial future. In early 2019, the Cairncross Review in the UK was published, which acknowledged the existential threat the digital business models of the online giants posed to traditional media owners. One of the recommendations put forward by the review panel was the formation of an Institute for Public-Interest News (Mayhew, 2019). According to the enquiry's chair, Dame Frances Cairncross, the proposed institute should:

> ensure complete freedom from any political or commercial obligations, and its strategic objective would be to ensure the future provision of public-interest news. It would become a centre of excellence and good practice, carrying out or commissioning research, building partnerships with universities, and developing the intellectual basis for measures to improve the accessibility and readership of quality news online.
>
> *(Mayhew, 2019)*

At the heart of this is a concern that expensive and often difficult investigative journalism performed in the public interest will not be economically viable in a fragmented media world. Although news providers do use Google and Facebook as channels to distribute much of their content, they are competing with much other content in this transient stream of news and are not able to maintain their distinct audiences and voices as they can on their own platforms. Although it is in Google and Facebook's interest to have access to a ready supply of third-party content, their business models are not configured to be content creators and there is little

42 Data generation and use in the 21st century

sign that this will change. We shall return to the regulatory implications of this shift in the media landscape in later sections but in the next chapter we will go deeper into the ways that data is being used to build new business models across a range of other sectors.

References

Alden, C. (2005, March 10). Looking Back on the Crash. *The Guardian*. www.theguardian.com/technology/2005/mar/10/newmedia.media.

Alphabet (2019). *Alphabet Investor Relations*. https://abc.xyz/.

Battelle, J. (2006). *The Search: How Google and its Rivals Rewrote the Rules of Business and Transformed Our Culture*. Nicholas Brealey Publishing.

BBC News (2000, April 27). Mobile Phone Auction Nets Billions. http://news.bbc.co.uk/1/hi/business/727831.stm.

Berners-Lee, T. & Fischetti, M. (1999). *Weaving the Web: The Original Design and Ultimate Destiny of the World Wide Web by Its Inventor*. Harper.

Casserly, M. (2019, February 8). Which is the More Popular Platform: iPhone or Android? Macworld UK. www.macworld.co.uk/feature/iphone/iphone-vs-android-market-share-3691861/.

CB Insights (2019a). *Amazon Strategy Teardown*. CB Insights. www.cbinsights.com/research/report/amazon-strategy-teardown/.

CB Insights (2019b). *Apple in Healthcare*. CB Insights. www.cbinsights.com/research/apple-healthcare-strategy-apps/.

Costello, S. (2019, May 30). How Many iPhones Have Been Sold Worldwide? Lifewire. www.lifewire.com/how-many-iphones-have-been-sold-1999500.

Deloitte (2017). *The Data Landscape* (p. 44). www2.deloitte.com/uk/en/pages/technology-media-and-telecommunications/articles/the-data-landscape.html.

Facebook (2019). Facebook Reports Fourth Quarter and Full Year 2018 Results. https://investor.fb.com/investor-news/press-release-details/2019/Facebook-Reports-Fourth-Quarter-and-Full-Year-2018-Results/default.aspx.

Galloway, S. (2018). *The Four: The Hidden DNA of Amazon, Apple, Facebook and Google*. Penguin Random House.

Google (2019). About Google. www.google.com/intl/en-GB/.

Internet Live Stats (2019). Total Number of Websites. www.internetlivestats.com/total-number-of-websites/.

Jackson, J. (2015, April 10). National Daily Newspaper Sales Fall by Half a Million in a Year. *The Guardian*. www.theguardian.com/media/2015/apr/10/national-daily-newspapers-lose-more-than-half-a-million-readers-in-past-year.

Johnson, L. (2016, July 25). Here's a Timeline of Yahoo's 22-Year History as a Digital Pioneer. AdWeek. www.adweek.com/digital/heres-timeline-yahoo-s-22-year-history-digital-pioneer-172663/.

Katz, M.L. & Shapiro, C. (1985). Network Externalities, Competition, and Compatibility. *American Economic Review*, 75(3), 424–440.

Leiner, B.M., Cerf, V.G., Clark, D.D., Kahn, R.E., Kleinrock, L., Lynch, D.C., Postel, J., Roberts, L.G. & Wolff, S. (2009). A Brief History of the Internet. *SIGCOMM Computer Communication Review*, 39(5), 22–31.

Lewis, P. (1994, April 10). Doubts Raised on Number of Internet Users. *The New York Times*. www.nytimes.com/1994/08/10/business/business-technology-doubts-raised-on-number-of-internet-users.html.

Mayhew, F. (2019, February 11). Cairncross Review: Institute for Public-Interest News, Innovation Fund and Tax Reliefs among Nine Proposals to Save UK News Industry. *Press Gazette*. www.pressgazette.co.uk/cairncross-review-institute-for-public-interest-news-innovation-fund-and-tax-reliefs-among-nine-proposals-to-save-uk-news-industry/.

Ofcom (2019). Advertising Expenditure. www.ofcom.org.uk/research-and-data/multi-sector-research/cmr/interactive-data.

Perez, C. (2003). *Technological Revolutions and Financial Capital: The Dynamics of Bubbles and Golden Ages*. Edward Elgar.

Planes, A. (2013, August 9). The IPO That Inflated the Dot-Com Bubble. The Motley Fool. www.fool.com/investing/general/2013/08/09/the-ipo-that-inflated-the-dot-com-bubble.aspx.

Ram, A. (2018, October 23). How 1m Apps are Tracking Users and Sharing their Data. *Financial Times*. https://ig.ft.com/mobile-app-data-trackers/.

Reimer, J. (2005, December 15). Total Share: 30 Years of Personal Computer Market Share Figures. Ars Technica. https://arstechnica.com/features/2005/12/total-share/.

Schroeder, W. (2016). *Germany's Industry 4.0 Strategy*. Friedrich Ebert Stiftung.

Segarra, L.M. (2018, September 29). Google to Pay Apple $12B to Remain Safari's Default Search Engine. Fortune. https://fortune.com/2018/09/29/google-apple-safari-search-engine/.

Soper, S. (2018, June 13). Amazon's Clever Machines Are Moving From the Warehouse to Headquarters. Bloomberg. https://bloom.bg/2Wyh6bw.

Statcounter (2019). Mobile Operating System Market Share Worldwide. StatCounter Global Stats. http://gs.statcounter.com/os-market-share/mobile/worldwide.

Statista (2019a). Facebook Users Worldwide 2019. www.statista.com/statistics/264810/number-of-monthly-active-facebook-users-worldwide/.

Statista (2019b). Smart Home – United Kingdom, Statista Market Forecast. www.statista.com/outlook/279/156/smart-home/united-kingdom.

Statista (2019c, February 26). Cell Phone Sales Worldwide 2007–2018. www.statista.com/statistics/263437/global-smartphone-sales-to-end-users-since-2007/.

Zenith (2018, November 19). 65% of Digital Media to be Programmatic in 2019. www.zenithmedia.com/65-of-digital-media-to-be-programmatic-in-2019/.

Zittrain, J. (2008). *The Future of the Internet*. Penguin Books.

4

EMERGING BUSINESS MODELS OF DATA-DRIVEN COMPANIES

Why business models matter

The notion of the business model is a relatively recent idea that has been developed by business academics and consultants to help explain how a business operates and why some are more successful than others. In essence, a business model describes what the business does, how it does this and how it generates revenues and profits. Teece (2010) offers a succinct definition of the term which fits well with the conclusions of many other commentators.

> The essence of a business model is in defining the manner by which the enterprise delivers value to customers, entices customers to pay for value, and converts those payments to profit. It thus reflects management's hypothesis about what customers want, how they want it, and how the enterprise can organize to best meet those needs, get paid for doing so, and make a profit.
>
> *(Teece, 2010, p. 172)*

At a practical level, the business model concept allows managers to segment a firm's activities and, if necessary, rearrange them to suit changing markets and technologies. This modular approach to understanding the activities of a firm has been adopted by Osterwalder and Pigneur (2010) and resulted in their Business Model Canvas tool that can be used to analyse, describe and design business models. Their work expands Teece's definition of the concept and breaks the activities of the firm into nine core components from defining customer needs and the firm's value proposition in response to those needs, to revenue streams and cost structures. Figure 4.1 shows these nine key elements of the Business Model Canvas and how they relate to each other.

46 New data-driven companies

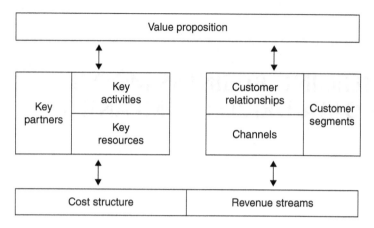

FIGURE 4.1 The Business Model Canvas, adapted from Osterwalder and Pigneur (2010)

The use of the business model as a conceptual tool to help entrepreneurs and managers build and run successful firms is important because it provides an abstract framework from which to plan a range of activities. Its use forces managers to think about all the processes that their company will need to engage with if it is to attract customers and deliver products or services that the market requires. At the heart of all successful business models is an expression of how value will be created and delivered to customers in a way that will provide a profit for the firm. As consumers become more sophisticated in their tastes and expectations and new distribution channels such as the internet offer innovative ways to deliver value, the design of business models becomes more important for firms that want to differentiate themselves from competitors. Companies that choose not to or are not able to adapt to these changes will fall behind and, as we are seeing across a range of sectors, eventually fail. Teece (2010) offers several historical precedents for industries that were transformed when new business models were developed and implemented by innovative firms. One of these examples dates back to nineteenth-century America, when Swift and Company reconfigured the way that meat was transported from Midwestern towns such as Kansas and Chicago to the rapidly growing consumer markets on the East Coast. Traditionally the cattle had been transported to their final destinations and then slaughtered and butchered and offered for sale to consumers. Swift and Company realised that the development of refrigerated railroad cars and warehouses would allow the cattle to be slaughtered, butchered and dressed before being transported to the East Coast, providing massive economies of scale resulting in cheaper meat for consumers. While this resulted in large profits for Swift and Company, it laid waste to many of the localised butchers and slaughterhouses that were reliant on the old system.

Other prominent examples of business model innovation transforming industries include the development of container shipping in the 1950s and 1960s and the rise of low-cost airlines in the 1980s and 1990s. The use of standardised metal containers that could be stacked efficiently on ships and then moved by crane directly onto specially adapted lorries dramatically reduced the labour costs traditionally associated with loading and unloading ships as well increasing the throughput of ports and speed of delivery. More recently, the airline industry has been impacted by the rise of low-cost carriers that offer no-frills direct flights between destinations rather than the traditional hub-and-spoke model of larger airlines that relied on changeovers at major airports before taking passengers to smaller cities.

Perhaps the most often-cited business model innovation is the razor-and-blade strategy often ascribed to the Gillette Company. This approach has been adopted by a number of other industries over the last 100 years and centres around offering consumers a low-cost or subsidised product that locks them into buying more expensive complementary products or services in the future. With razors, the razor itself is sold very cheaply while the replacement blades are more expensive. The proprietary nature of the fitting system and the use of intellectual property law means that consumers can only buy the blades from one supplier. This model has worked well for Gillette and Wilkinson for many years, although it is interesting that new models in this sector are now emerging. These centre on a subscription model where new blades are sent directly to consumers on a regular basis. The fundamental change in the razor business model with the subscription service is the nature of the relationship between the manufacturer and the consumer; the relationship is much closer, with the razor maker knowing the name and address of its customers, offering the potential for marketing and selling other products and services.

The rise of digital channels for marketing and sales has provided new opportunities for business model innovations. The economics of digital distribution, as we shall see in a later section, allows for more flexibility in revenue models as marginal distribution costs in a digital world fall to nearly zero. So-called freemium models for software and content distribution have become popular in recent years as a way to entice customers with free but limited, often ad-supported services with the expectation that some of them will upgrade to a premium package at a later date. In the next section, the impact of data-driven business models across a range of sectors will be examined with a focus on the rise of technology platforms.

Data-driven business models

Just as the innovations of mechanisation in the nineteenth century and information technology in the twentieth century led to new business models, so the generation and use of data in the twenty-first century is giving rise to new configurations of business processes and service models. The Industrial Revolution created a middle class and spawned mass consumption. The Communications Revolution a century later resulted in mass audiences, driving the rise of branded products and global fast-moving consumer goods (FMCG) companies such as Proctor and Gamble,

Unilever and Nestle. These companies established sophisticated, global supply chains that transformed the logistics industry. Their size enabled massive economies of scale which, in conjunction with the rise of supermarkets, forced many smaller competitors from the marketplace when they could not compete either on price or consumer reach. While much of the twentieth century's corporate battles were fought over access to physical resources and the exploitation of scale and purchasing power, the current century is seeing an additional dimension that firms will have to deal with: data. Size may still be important for firms as they compete on a global stage, but what they do with the data they generate from their activities is also crucial.

A 2015 survey conducted by the Economist Intelligence Unit (EIU) of 476 executives across a range of industries in the US, EU and Asia found that 83% had used data to make existing products and services more profitable and 69% believed there was a case for creating a new business unit focused on building data-related products or services (EIU, 2015). In this sense, we can see that data is becoming a crucial input to business development and, for many firms, a driving force for business model innovation. These changes reflect the rise of data generation and the ability of firms to analyse these new information streams through the application of cheaper and more effective computing technologies. It is important to note that it is not just digitally native companies such as Google and Facebook that are exploiting this new resource. Established industry incumbents are also making use of the data they generate through their everyday business activities, as the OECD noted in a recent report.

> Even traditional sectors such as retail are changing: firms like Tesco, the UK supermarket chain, exploit huge data flows generated through their fidelity card programmes. The Tesco programme now counts more than 100 market baskets a second and 6 million transactions a day, and it very effectively transformed Tesco from a local, downmarket 'pile 'em high, sell 'em cheap' retailer to a multinational, customer-oriented one with broad appeal across social groups.
>
> *(OECD, 2013, p. 4)*

As technology becomes cheaper and more accessible, new entrants are able to capitalise on building businesses in niche areas where data capture and manipulation takes a central role in their business models. In many ways, these smaller firms have an advantage in that they are not encumbered with legacy systems and processes that can slow down industry incumbents. This has become apparent in the financial services sector where customers of a number of large banks have had their services severely disrupted as the firms have updated back-office systems, some of which were developed in the 1970s. Innovative new entrants are able to build systems that can take advantage of channels such as the internet and end-points such as smartphones that are more efficient and cost-effective than expensive physical branch networks and outdated software.

A common feature of many of these new firms using data at the heart of their business models is the development of platforms to offer a more compelling proposition to consumers as well as to provide a competitive advantage over rivals. A recent survey of 2,320 European small and medium-sized enterprises (SMEs) that were developing digital platforms found that more than two-thirds were less than ten years old, with almost half having been formed in the previous five years (De Marco et al., 2019). The use of platforms by internet companies such as Google and Facebook was considered in the previous chapter but it is important to note that smaller companies are also using the advantages of a platform-based business model to attract and retain customers. At the heart of many of these platforms is the building of communities of stakeholders that can share data in a mutually beneficial way. Some of the core research into platform strategies is considered in a later section but in the context of data-driven business models a platform approach can provide an environment that makes the best commercial use of the data captured by a firm. We have seen how Google has done this with search data and Facebook with social connection data, building platforms that harness this data for advertising purposes. As these platforms grow and third-party firms build products and services around them, it becomes more difficult for new entrants to build competing services as they are locked out of the dominant ecosystem.

As increasing volumes of data are generated through business processes and consumer activity, all sectors of developed economies are being affected. The marketing and advertising sectors have been at the forefront of these changes since the late 1990s but as the Internet of Things (IoT) permeates other industries and activities, we can expect to see data being used to disrupt existing business processes and create new value for firms and consumers. One of the largest and most profitable data markets is in the financial sector. Global spending on financial market data by banks and investment firms totalled $28.5 billion in 2017. One of the most successful firms offering such data is Bloomberg, which launched its first Bloomberg Terminals to financial institutions in New York in 1982. Since then the company's terminals and information services have become a fixture on over 320,000 traders' desks around the world, each paying approximately $24,000 annually for the privilege (CB Insights, 2018b). However, new entrants offering less expensive and less feature-rich services have emerged since the financial crisis of 2008, which do not rely on dedicated terminals and provide 'good enough' data services to clients. While the Bloomberg platform has locked in customers for several decades, the ease of access to data provided by the internet threatens this model. The economics of information as outlined in the following section makes competition in established and emerging data-driven markets a more complex and fast-moving phenomena – as Bloomberg is discovering.

The economics of data

Data, unlike most other commodities used by firms to generate profits, has some unique characteristics that provide opportunities for businesses but also present

50 New data-driven companies

challenges. This is particularly true with digitised data, where replication and distribution is almost cost-free and instantaneous. In economics this is often referred to as a non-rivalrous good in that the use of data by one person or organisation does not prevent its use by another, as opposed to physical commodities such as coal, steel or electricity. Thomas Jefferson, one of the Founding Fathers of the United States and the third American president, described it more eloquently in a letter in 1813.

> He who receives an idea from me, receives instruction himself without lessening mine; as he who lights his taper at mine, receives light without darkening me.
>
> *(Darnton, 2011)*

This is not to say that information or data is, therefore, a free commodity. Jefferson's taper cost real money to make and purchase and much information is expensive to produce. The distinguishing feature is in the replication and distribution where, with a newspaper article or movie, for example, there may be high up-front costs of production but subsequent copies can be shared at a near-zero marginal cost and without preventing others from also reading the article or watching the film. In their seminal text on the pricing of digital goods, Shapiro and Varian (1998) explore these dynamics and present a range of examples illustrating the challenges that information providers from the analogue and paper age had to face with the rise of digital technologies since the 1980s. A pertinent example is that of the *Encyclopaedia Britannica*, which first started publishing its multi-volume reference work in the eighteenth century. By the early 1990s this had grown into 32 volumes which cost approximately $1,600. In 1992, Microsoft decided it needed to produce CD-ROM content to encourage home sales of PCs running its Windows operating system. Central to this was an encyclopaedia with multimedia content that would fit on a CD-ROM. To this end, it bought the rights to the print encyclopaedia of Funk and Wagnalls, a minor competitor to *Britannica* that was sold in supermarkets. The resulting CD version was sold for $49.95 to consumers, with many PC manufacturers bundling it free with their computers. Very quickly the *Britannica's* market share began to fall as consumers found the quality of Microsoft's Encarta satisfactory for most of their needs and the price very attractive. The *Britannica* responded with a CD version of its own which it sold on a subscription basis to libraries for $2,000 per year. However, the company's market share continued to fall and by 1996 its revenues had halved from their 1990 level (Shapiro and Varian, 1998). Aggressive price cutting followed but the company was not able to successfully adapt to this new digital landscape. The *Britannica's* costs in paying experts to create the content for its product could not be covered in a world where reference information was becoming commoditised. The company limped on for a number of years but announced in 2012 that it would no longer produce its print edition, ironically lasting three years longer than its rival Encarta, which ceased production of CDs in 2009 (De Saulles, 2015). Just as the *Encyclopaedia Britannica* struggled to adapt to the age of the CD-ROM, so Encarta could not compete in the almost friction-free world of the internet and the WWW. Wikipedia has surpassed them both as the most popular reference source by offering a free model to consumers that relies on unpaid volunteers and contributors to create its content.

For firms and entrepreneurs planning to build businesses around data, it is important that the economics of information are understood. Central to this is an appreciation of the difference between fixed and variable costs in a data-driven business. As a general rule, the fixed costs of production in a data-driven business are high but the variable costs of reproduction are small. As Shapiro and Varian (1998) describe it, the fixed costs are sunk costs in that they are not recoverable should production be halted. These sunk costs are generally paid up-front and need to be factored in to the pricing of the final digital product. However, there are some exceptions to this rule which have been enabled by the rise of the internet, the WWW and social media. As already mentioned, Wikipedia makes use of a largely unpaid workforce to create its content and, despite early misgivings by many commentators, is able to produce a reference source that is generally trusted. By using a crowd-sourcing approach to content generation, errors and fraudulent entries are discovered quickly and corrected. While many researchers and academics argue that Wikipedia is a good starting point for finding information rather than the final source, it is still a surprisingly successful and cost-effective model of information creation. Another exception to Shapiro and Varian's description of information-based businesses having high fixed costs and low variable costs is Facebook. While the company has significant costs associated with running its infrastructure, most of the content it relies on is generated for free by its user base. So-called user-generated content (UGC) has also been very profitably harnessed by YouTube with uploaded videos and by Google with web content which it indexes but does not create.

Another exception to the high-fixed-costs rule can be seen with companies that use data generated by public-sector bodies and which is made freely available for commercial reuse through government policy. Large datasets created by federal government bodies in the US have been made accessible for these purposes for a number of decades and a similar approach is now being taken in the UK and across the EU. Part of the rationale for this strategy rests in the belief that as taxpayers have already paid for the collection of this data to help with the efficient running of government, it is only fair that the data should be freely available in ways that can benefit the economy. The types of data available typically include meteorological information and census, transportation and statistical data on the economy. While the UK has experimented with charging firms for access to some datasets, the EU has introduced policies aimed at creating a dynamic market in data reuse by providing free access within member states. For firms this can be a valuable resource that lowers their cost base and as government portals offering access to public data grow in size and scope, they offer the potential for driving a number of data-driven innovations and businesses. By late 2019 the UK's data.gov.uk portal was offering free access to more than 59,000 datasets, while the US's data.gov offered almost

52 New data-driven companies

253,000. However, while open data from public sources can be used to create a range of value-added services, it also lowers the barriers to entry for start-ups wishing to build data-driven businesses. All firms have equal access to the same data and so competitive advantage lies with how that data is processed, combined with other information and, very often, built into a platform offering that provides a dynamic ecosystem which others would find difficult to replicate. The next section considers some of the approaches taken by firms as they design and build data-driven businesses.

Emerging data-driven business models

As discussed in the previous two chapters, companies have been building businesses around the capture, processing and selling of data for more than 100 years. However, the Computing and Internet Revolution has presented new opportunities for firms to use data. We have seen how some of the world's largest and most profitable companies have created empires around the exploitation of internet-generated data, primarily based on creating advertising platforms. This section considers the use of technology platforms as a strategy to build sustainable data-driven businesses and presents some examples of the innovative business models being developed by firms across a range of sectors.

The use of platforms by firms around which to build a business or product line can be traced back over 100 years. Henry Ford and later automobile manufacturers built ranges of car models around common components and vehicle frames or chassis. This approach provided a cost-effective way of launching new models without having to redesign the entire car each time as well as offering economies of scale at the production level. Gawer and Cusumano (2002) describe these as internal platforms in that a company uses them as the basis for its own future products or service development. In their extensive studies on platform strategies, the two authors also describe external industry platforms as:

> products, services, or technologies that are similar in some ways to the former but provide the foundation upon which outside firms (organized as a 'business ecosystem') can develop their own complementary products, technologies, or services.
>
> *(Gawer and Cusumano, 2014, p. 418)*

The external platform strategy has been used to great effect by some of the largest technology companies over the previous 30 years, including Microsoft, Intel, Cisco, Google and Apple. These companies have built 'business ecosystems', as described by Gawer and Cusumano, from which many outside firms have been able to offer their own products and services to complement the core offering from the platform originator. During the personal computer (PC) revolution of the 1980s and 1990s, Microsoft and Intel led the development of the PC platform and were the largest beneficiaries of the profits generated as a result. Microsoft controlled the software platform of the PC through its ownership of MS-DOS and Windows, while Intel led the design and development of the hardware architecture around the central processing unit (CPU). The two companies allowed their central components to be open enough that third-party companies could build software to run on MS-DOS or Windows and be compatible with the CPU architecture as well as hardware that would be compatible with these systems. As a result, developers of business and consumer software and producers of monitors, hard drives, keyboards and other peripherals including assembled PCs were able to create profitable businesses in their own niches. Consumers benefited by having a wider range of options to choose from when buying a PC. This became a virtuous circle of innovation and sales as developers were attracted to a platform that had a rapidly growing number of consumers and PC buyers were drawn in by the product choices on offer. Conversely, Apple Computers during this period saw its share of the personal computing market fall as it adopted a more proprietary approach whereby it built and sold the computer and the core software for its product range. While Apple Mac computers were popular with users, the lack of choices on offer in terms of third-party software and hardware made them less attractive to new computer buyers. Central to the commercial success of such external technology platforms is the leadership of their originators and the degree to which they keep the platform open to outside developers. Control is important to ensure the trajectory of development is consistent but there needs to be sufficient flexibility that encourages outside firms to build complementary products and services with the expectation of receiving a profitable return. Google has achieved this with its Android mobile operating system where, although the software is open-source, the company has set rules about how it can be implemented if other Google services such as the app store or maps are to be integrated. While this approach is coming under closer regulatory scrutiny around the world due to Google's dominant market share of the smartphone OS market, it has proven extremely successful in creating a dynamic ecosystem for hardware and software developers.

The success of both the Android and the iOS software platforms has been instrumental in driving a new generation of platforms where data has played a key role in creating value for the consumers and the developers. In a number of cases the essence of the business models behind these companies is using data and analytics to more efficiently match up supply and demand across a variety of sectors. Ride-hailing firms such as Uber and Lyft have done this successfully in the market for taxi services. Typically, customers wanting a ride in major cities would stand on the street and wait for a taxi to drive past and hail it down. This was inefficient for the consumer in that they may have faced a long wait before an available car passed by them, and less-than-optimal for the driver who would have to drive around the city until they found a passenger. As a result, demand often went unmet and the supply side was not used efficiently, with empty cars roaming the streets. Uber, Lyft and other similar firms around the world made good use of the rise of mass, always-connected smartphones, their location awareness and the open app stores to offer a way for consumers to instantly signal their desire for a taxi without having

54 New data-driven companies

to explain where they wanted to be picked up from. On top of this, the ability for drivers and customers to rate each other via the app and a cashless payment system has resulted in shorter waits and more efficiently used cars. The data generated through app usage allows the operators to implement dynamic pricing strategies that vary with demand as well as helping drivers select routes and times that optimise their working hours. These types of high-growth and demand-matching apps have been referred to as hyperscale platforms that can be extended to smooth out inefficiencies in resource allocation across markets beyond their original target. In the case of ride-hailing apps, the consulting firm McKinsey and Co., which coined the term 'hyperscale', sees this data-driven approach being used for driverless cars.

> Autonomous vehicles, which appear to be on the horizon, could accelerate this wave of change. When self-driving cars are added into the equation, supply and demand matching could improve even further since these vehicles can have higher utilization rates. Car-pooling may increase, and the cost of urban transportation could plummet. On the flip side, the demand for car purchases could fall further, and many people who make a living as drivers (nearly two million in the United States alone with the majority being truck drivers) could be displaced.
>
> *(McKinsey & Co., 2016, p. 61)*

There are obvious social and economic implications of these changes should McKinsey's predictions prove true. These may be positive in terms of lower pollution in cities and fewer road deaths, but the resulting restructuring of an automotive industry built around mass car sales to consumers could lead to higher unemployment. However, as with many previous innovations, the attraction of high profits from the new entrants may prove to be unstoppable and a long period of social adjustment may be required. Similar patterns are emerging in other market sectors where the application of data analytics to take out inefficiencies in established business practices is resulting in the development of innovative business models.

Insurance companies have used data to help calculate risk and estimate appropriate charges for customers for many years. In the life insurance market, age has been a core factor in determining premiums, with younger policy holders typically paying less than older ones, whose probability of dying is far higher. Automobile insurance follows an inverse model where younger drivers are statistically more likely to be involved in an accident and therefore pay more than safer, older car owners. Other factors such as occupation and the answers to lifestyle questionnaires also feed into the risk calculations but the methodology has changed little throughout most of the twentieth century. However, new entrants into the insurance sector as well as some industry incumbents are drawing on far wider sources of data in their risk models. In the case of life and medical insurance this data may come from fitness trackers worn by consumers as well as more general social media platforms where lifestyle information may be inferred from postings and likes. Although use of such data is not the norm, as far as researchers can tell, in 2019 it does seem to be on the increase according to Scism (2019), who looked at evidence from the US. She presents a list of *do*s and *don't*s for anyone worried about the data a medical or life insurer may use in calculating their premium.

> Don't post photos of yourself smoking on social-media sites;
>
> Do post photos of yourself running. Riskier sports, like skydiving, could complicate the situation.
>
> Use fitness-tracking devices that indicate an interest in fitness.
>
> Purchase food from online meal-preparation services that specialize in healthy choices.
>
> Visit the gym with a phone linked to a location-tracking service. If you visit the bar, leave your phone at home.
>
> *(Scism, 2019)*

While social media posts may be public and easily accessible to insurers to scrape and analyse, data from fitness trackers is far less public. Users of fitness apps often have the option to make feeds of their activity such as runs or cycle rides public but most people choose to keep this data private. However, from the perspective of insurance providers, granular health data such as activity levels, heart rate, blood pressure and body weight is far more valuable than inferred calculations from social media data. To this end, a number of firms are offering wearable fitness trackers to consumers with the promise of lower premiums for those demonstrating healthy lifestyles. Founded in Switzerland in 2010, dacadoo has built a platform which uses gaming techniques and AI to collect health data from wearables for use by the insurance sector. The company does not sell its own fitness trackers or apps to consumers but is agnostic in that its platform can work with many vendors and developers. Insurers are able to 'white label' the platform to their customers with dacadoo sitting in the background collecting the data and applying a proprietary 'health score' to it. The company's score uses the real-time and historical data being generated by connected fitness apps, smart watches, interactive scales, activity trackers and blood pressure monitors to produce a value from 1 to 1,000 (CB Insights, 2018a). This platform-based business model does not rely on building an entire system of hardware and software to capture and analyse data but rather utilises the products already used by consumers in the marketplace and adds value through its processing and analysis.

While the insurance sector adapts to a new world of real-time health and life-style data, other industries are also seeing the emergence of new businesses and business models that draw on the increasing volumes of consumer data becoming available. In the banking sector, changes to financial regulations in the EU are opening up customer data to third parties from which they can create new services and companies. The Payment Services Directive 2 (PSD2) which came into force across EU member states in 2018 allows bank customers to share data about their transactions with other providers via secure IT systems (Vila, 2019). In the UK, a number of start-ups have created apps and services on top of this data. Credit Kudos provides a free service to customers which analyses their financial data and spending patterns to calculate credit scores and eligibility for different financial services. Money Dashboard pulls customers' financial data into a single digital dashboard and helps users better understand spending patterns and offers help with techniques to save money. Other apps and companies such as Flux, Trussle and Plum offer similar services that analyse financial data from users and help them secure better deals with mortgages, loyalty schemes and loans. The key factor in unlocking the potential of this data lies with the regulatory approach adopted by the EU, which saw the established banking sector as a roadblock to innovation. As traditional industries adapt to the emerging data-driven landscape we can expect to see more initiatives and regulations aimed at opening up sectors resistant to change.

While the banking and insurance sectors and their traditional reliance on data to deliver services may seem natural areas for data-driven innovation, there are other less-obvious markets where innovative uses of data are creating new businesses. The legal sector has seen a number of new entrants offering data analysis services to help clients select lawyers, applying AI techniques to the analysis of corporate documents as well as helping legal professionals find reliable expert witnesses (Reed, 2019).

The rise of football analytics is another area attracting attention and substantial investments. Sporting data has long been used by coaches, managers and the betting industry to predict likely winners and identify areas of improvement for teams and athletes. Football has been one of the more difficult sports from which to collect and analyse data due to the speed of the game, number of players on the pitch and possible permutations of play. However, firms such as Opta Sports now employ teams of event-coders who use technology to record the time and location of every pass, dribble, shot and tackle, with an average match containing approximately 2,000 data points (Burn-Murdoch, 2018). From this data, predictions about expected results and performance data for individual players can be calculated, helping bookmakers calculate odds and managers select players most appropriate to their needs.

In the world of high fashion, data capture and analysis with AI techniques is also emerging as a source of competitive advantage for brands and retailers. Italian firm YNAP, an amalgamation of Yoox and Net-a-Porter in 2015, owns a range of online, upmarket fashion retail sites. Its more-than-5,000 employees and estimated annual sales of over $2 billion make it a major destination for consumers looking for the latest styles from major brands. What makes the company interesting is the way it combines the traditional skills of its experienced buyers whose experiences of market tastes and trends inform their decisions with cutting-edge data capture and analysis. The company sees the application of data processing as central to its success and as a way of differentiating itself from competitors in the ruthless online retail space. In 2019, the company's CEO Federico Marchetti outlined this approach.

> We sit on a gold mine of data. We have 3 million high spenders around the world who we can serve through data better and better and better through personalisation.

> *(McDowell, 2019)*

Much of the data collected by the company is used to predict likely sales of product ranges to help prevent over or under-buying as well as helping buyers choose products likely to be popular with customers. While AI techniques have been applied to help with this process, the buyers and managers have a power of veto over any automated decisions which they feel are not realistic. This may point the way to the future for many firms involved in the creative sectors where predicting human behaviour may always be part-science and part-art. Technology may have an important role in helping with the decision making process but will not always hold the complete answer.

Finally, the value of data to power new business models in far-from-obvious sectors is well illustrated with robotic vacuum cleaners. While their core benefit to consumers is one of labour and time saving, for the companies making the cleaners, data may provide a valuable revenue stream. Homes are complex areas to navigate in terms of the furniture and other obstacles placed around rooms. By its nature, a robotic vacuum cleaner has to map this terrain to avoid bumping into or knocking over objects. According to the company's CEO:

> There's an entire ecosystem of things and services that the smart home can deliver once you have a rich map of the home that the user has allowed to be shared.
>
> *(Wolfe, 2017)*

Possible uses of this data include audio systems that could adjust their acoustics to suit the conditions in specific rooms and smart lighting that could adjust itself to window positioning and time of day, as well as helping makers of other smart home devices such as Amazon and Google to recommend home products to buy. While these are niche uses and unlikely to lead to multi-billion business opportunities, they illustrate the creative uses to which seemingly valueless data can be put. They also raise questions about privacy and the extent to which many of these businesses rely on personal data to generate value. These questions are considered in the next chapter as well as possible solutions, both regulatory and technological.

References

Burn-Murdoch, J. (2018, November 1). How Data Analysis Helps Football Clubs Make Better Signings. *Financial Times*. www.ft.com/content/84aa8b5e-c1a9-11e8-84cd-9e601db069b8.

CB Insights. (2018a). *Quarterly InsurTech Briefing*. CB Insights.

CB Insights. (2018b). *Twilight of the Terminal: The Disruption of Bloomberg L.P.* CB Insights.

Darnton, R. (2011, November 24). Jefferson's Taper: A National Digital Library. *The New York Review of Books*. www.nybooks.com/articles/2011/11/24/jeffersons-taper-national-digital-library/.

De Marco, C., Di Minin, A., Marullo, C. & Nepelski, D. (2019). *Digital Platform Innovation in European SMEs* (JRC Technical Reports). European Commission.

De Saulles, M. (2015). *Information 2.0: New Models of Information Production, Distribution and Consumption* (2nd edn). Facet Publishing.

EIU (2015). *The Business of Data. Economist* Intelligence Unit.

Gawer, A. & Cusumano, M.A. (2002). *Platform Leadership: How Intel, Microsoft and Cisco Drive Industry Innovation.* Harvard Business School Press.

Gawer, A. & Cusumano, M.A. (2014). Industry Platforms and Ecosystem Innovation. *Journal of Product Innovation Management, 31*(3), 417–433.

McDowell, M. (2019, July 3). Yoox Net-a-Porter CEO: 'We Sit On a Gold Mine of Data'. *Vogue Business.* www.voguebusiness.com/companies/yoox-net-a-porter-ceo-federico-marchetti-ynap.

McKinsey & Co. (2016). *The Age of Analytics: Competing in a Data-Driven World* (p. 136). www.mckinsey.com/business-functions/mckinsey-analytics/our-insights/the-age-of-analytics-competing-in-a-data-driven-world.

OECD (2013). Exploring Data-Driven Innovation as a New Source of Growth: Mapping the Policy Issues Raised by Big Data (OECD Digital Economy Papers, p. 44). http://dx.doi.org/10.1787/5k47zw3fcp43-en.

Osterwalder, A. & Pigneur, Y. (2010). *Business Model Generation: A Handbook for Visionaries, Game Changers, and Challengers* (1st edn). John Wiley & Sons.

Reed, N. (2019, January 15). Legal Analytics, The Next Frontier: How the Data-Driven Lawyer is Becoming Reality. Legal Tech News. www.law.com/legaltechnews/2019/01/15/legal-analytics-the-next-frontier-how-the-data-driven-lawyer-is-becoming-reality/?slreturn=20190507102932.

Scism, L. (2019, January 30). New York Insurers Can Evaluate Your Social Media Use—If They Can Prove Why It's Needed. *The Wall Street Journal.* www.wsj.com/articles/new-york-insurers-can-evaluate-your-social-media-useif-they-can-prove-why-its-needed-11548856802.

Shapiro, C. & Varian, H.R. (1998). *Information Rules: A Strategic Guide to the Network Economy.* Harvard Business Review Press.

Teece, D.J. (2010). Business Models, Business Strategy and Innovation. *Long Range Planning, 43*(2–3), 172–194.

Vila, C.T. (2019, June 3). We Should Extend EU Bank Data Sharing to All Sectors. *Financial Times.* www.ft.com/content/0304b078-82c6-11e9-a7f0-77d3101896ec.

Wolfe, J. (2017, July 28). Roomba Vacuum Maker iRobot Betting Big on the 'Smart' Home. Reuters. www.reuters.com/article/us-irobot-strategy-idUSKBN1A91A5.

5

CHALLENGES FOR POLICYMAKERS AND LAW MAKERS

Privacy in a world of data

The need for regulation

Earlier chapters have touched on some of the social and legal issues emerging from the data gathering efforts of some of the internet giants of the twenty-first century. This chapter explores in more detail recent cases of data infringement and the problems which have resulted. The limitations of current regulatory models are considered and potential alternatives are discussed. To set the scene, we will look at some of the higher-level reasons why regulation is a necessity in a world driven by data.

While many of the discussions around data gathering and personal privacy have understandably been focused on high-profile consumer-facing companies such as Google and Facebook, less attention has been paid to the companies operating in the background that collect and sell personal data: data brokers. There is no strict definition of what a data broker is but the Federal Trade Commission (FTC) in the US describes them as:

> companies that collect consumers' personal information and resell or share that information with others – [they] are important participants in this Big Data economy.
>
> *(FTC, 2014, p. i)*

In its study of the data broker industry in the US, the FTC identified nine key players that, between them, maintained extensive information on almost every consumer. One of the companies had data on 1.4 billion consumer transactions and more than 700 billion aggregated data elements. Another adds 3 billion new records to its database each month, while yet another has 3,000 different data points for nearly every US consumer (FTC, 2014). The data is collected from an assortment

60 Challenges for policy and law makers

of financial institutions, retailers, internet companies, public sources and marketing organisations. Some of the data brokers have their origins in the credit checking agencies discussed in Chapter 1, while others are more recent and focus on providing data to the marketing sector. The internet and smartphone revolutions have provided a fresh wave of data sources for these companies and a new generation of data brokers have emerged that seek to capture data on our searching, browsing and clicking behaviour. In 2010, *The Wall Street Journal* investigated these internet tracking brokers and found that the top 50 US websites which accounted for almost 40% of web browsing by Americans placed 3,180 tracking files on their test computer. While some of these trackers were innocuous, used to remember passwords or track page views, more than 2,200 were installed by 131 companies and used to create data bases of consumer profiles that could then be sold to interested parties (Angwin, 2010). These new data sources have created a dynamic new industry which is forecast to be worth as much as €106.8 billion in 2020 in Europe alone (Murgia and Ram, 2019).

Much of the information collected and sold by brokers is used by firms to make decisions on the credit-worthiness of individuals or to better target advertisements which, it could be argued, make for a better browsing experience. Many of the marketing-focused brokers create profiles of different consumer categories such as first-time home purchasers or recent retirees and then sell these profile groups to interested advertisers. However, sometimes these profile groups can be centred on more sensitive data such as racial identity or specific health issues. Some brokers specialise in specific sectors such as fitness tracking data or online dating activity. Problems arise may arise when the data is not anonymised, as happened in 2018 when Spanish researcher Joana Moll was able to buy the online dating profiles of 1 million people for €136 from the broker, USDate. The data included 5 million photographs, dates of birth, postal codes, genders and information on sexuality, religion, marital status and smoking and drinking habits (Murgia and Ram, 2019). While the USDate example may be the exception with many brokers claiming all their data is anonymised, there is a growing consensus that trying to make personal data anonymous is impossible, particularly when it contains location information. Researchers in Belgium and London have studied how easy it is to deanonymise any arbitary dataset and concluded that:

> A dataset with 15 demographic attributes, for instance, 'would render 99.98% of people in Massachusetts unique'. And for smaller populations, it gets easier: if town-level location data is included, for instance, 'it would not take much to reidentify people living in Harwich Port, Massachusetts, a city of fewer than 2,000 inhabitants'.
>
> *(Hern, 2019b)*

Bearing in mind that many data brokers sell 'anonymised' datasets on individuals and households with several hundred data points per entry, it is easy to see why campaigners, policymakers and regulators are concerned about this issue. As with many areas of law impacted by new technologies, regulators and law makers are always playing a game of catch-up, where the companies building the technologies that generate, capture, store and manipulate data are usually three steps ahead. The process of creating legislation is generally a slow one and with good reason. Haste often results in bad law as the potential impacts are not sufficiently considered and stakeholders are not allowed a voice in the drafting of legislation. As this chapter demonstrates, the rise of digital data has presented new challenges that did not exist in an analogue world. Data is generated far more quickly and at greater scale than ever before. Coupled with the ability to effortlessly replicate perfect copies and distribute them at virtually zero cost across national boundaries, controlling who does what with increasingly fluid data is becoming more difficult.

The history of regulation

Regulations on how data can be collected and used have multiplied over the last 50 years due to the rise of computing systems and, more recently, the internet. However, legislation relating to the use of information can be traced back much further. A legal case in the US in 1604 established the principle that 'the house of every one is to him his castle and fortress' and enforced the notion that this extended to personal privacy and the unsolicited capture of private conversations (Solove, 2016). Over 150 years there was growing concern in the US of government intrusion and the collection of personal information through searches of private residences. This concern was exacerbated with the first national census in 1790 which, by 1890, was asking questions about disabilities, diseases and finances, leading to a public outcry and legislation in 1919 by the US Congress outlining stricter rules for protecting the confidentiality of census data (Solove, 2016).

The rise of the telegraph and then the telephone in the nineteenth century saw the emergence of technologies to hack into these networks, initially by Union and Confederate armies trying to ascertain each other's battle plans and later by criminals wanting to know the results of sporting events and stock market movements before they could be reported in the newspapers (Standage, 1999). Laws were passed on both sides of the Atlantic to try and prevent these activities but, as with the fight against cyber crime today, the lawmakers were usually playing a game of catch-up.

In the post-war period in the US it was becoming apparent that public bodies were the largest collectors of data as part of their administrative duties. Pressure to make this data more freely available to aid public scrutiny of government activities led to the 1966 Freedom of Information Act, allowing any citizen to request records held by executive agencies. With exceptions for information relating to matters of security or sensitive medical records, this has established a principle of viewing public-sector information as a national asset. Over the last 40 years, a thriving industry has grown up in the US around the exploitation of public information assets and their repurposing into commercial products and services.

In the UK, information legislation of the first half of the twentieth century centred on restricting access to public information. Much of this was due to the

62 Challenges for policy and law makers

need for state secrecy spanning two world wars but, it could be argued, also reflected a cultural attitude dominant amongst those in power. Official Secrets legislation from the First World War established a default principle of secrecy for all activities of the state, something that did not change for decades. From the 1950s, the idea that a national information policy would be beneficial both socially and economically started to take root in the UK. According to Orna (2008):

> By 1970 most of the elements that make up the contemporary idea of national information policy had emerged: what governments tell their own population and those of other countries for their own policy purposes; protection of personal data and freedom of information; collection of statistical data for policy-making; and the use of ICT to manage and analyse information.
>
> *(Orna, 2008, p. 549)*

The diverse nature of Europe in terms of nation states and cultural habits and attitudes has seen a slower move to freeing up public-sector information. However, the rise of the EU as a common trading block and legislation around the collection and dissemination of public and private data assets has created a more dynamic environment. Just as EU policymakers and legislators see the need for common rules for the efficient trade of goods and services amongst member states, so the free transfer and sharing of information is seen as essential to support these activities. Since the early 1980s, several EU directives on data protection have been passed and enacted into the national laws of member states. The most recent of these is the General Data Protection Regulation (GDPR) of 2016 that sets strict rules on what types of information can be collected, for what purposes and under what conditions. The GDPR will be discussed in more detail in a later section but it is important to note that the legislation is symptomatic of a growing concern amongst regulators of illicit data use.

Other significant EU legislation has impacted on the re-use of public-sector information (RPSI) and copyright. Several rounds of RPSI legislation from the EU since 2003, culminating in a directive from 2019, have sought to stimulate the market for using public-sector information (PSI) to drive economic activity. The underlying principle views PSI as a public asset that should be made available for free or at the marginal cost of dissemination to any organisation or individual that wishes to repurpose it for commercial or social reasons. The most recent legislation, commonly referred to as the Open Data Directive (Directive (EU) 2019/1024), has introduced the principle of high-value datasets. These datasets are:

- geospatial
- earth observation and environment
- meteorological
- statistics
- companies and company ownership
- mobility

As a sign of their perceived importance they are:

> subject to a separate set of rules ensuring their availability free of charge, in machine readable formats, provided via Application Programming Interfaces (APIs) and, where relevant, as bulk download.
>
> *(European Commission, 2019)*

This legislation is significant in that it signals a growing demand amongst the private sector to have access to public data assets. Central to arguments around opening up public information resources is the notion that they were created with public funds and so should be used for the greater social good. Alongside this is the belief that the incentives of the marketplace and the skills of innovators suit the creation of information products that serve a public and commercial need. However, in some member states there are barriers to overcome culturally and at a technical level. Some public bodies have shown a reluctance to allow private companies access to their data as it goes against a tradition of state secrecy. There are also technical issues that many public bodies are struggling with in terms of providing robust and reliable APIs that meet the needs of commercial innovators.

Some of these issues are explored in the following sections.

Current regulatory models

As we have seen, the regulation of data and information products and services varies between countries due to cultural and commercial interests and pressures. The rise of the digital age has accelerated the demand for new laws to combat abuse of the mass collection of personal data as well as the illicit copying and sharing of intellectual property. Tied up with this are the competing interests of companies whose business models rely on the exploitation of data and nation states that seek to control information flows for political reasons.

As digital data is invisible it can flow seamlessly between national boundaries, bypassing the checks and inspections common with physical goods. This requires new forms of cooperation between government bodies to agree standards and rules for data sharing. However, it should be noted that concerns about the international trade in information-based products goes back more than 100 years. In the nineteenth century the British writer Charles Dickens and the American author Mark Twain were calling for new laws to prevent their books being illegally copied on opposite sides of the Atlantic. The Berne Convention of 1886 began a process of international alignment of copyright laws between industrialised economies with the US passing its own international copyright law in 1891. The wireless transmission of media content in the twentieth century followed by the growth of digital networks over the last 25 years has seen more international agreements aimed at preventing, with often limited success, the illegal sharing of copyrighted materials.

In 2020, there are several broad areas of dispute between nation states and trading blocks. In the EU there is a growing effort to curtail some of the powers

64 Challenges for policy and law makers

of the larger internet companies such as Google and Facebook with respect to the trading of personal data. The US-centric nature of much of the internet economy is increasingly coming into conflict with EU demands with politicians on both sides using data regulation as bargaining tools. This is being felt most acutely with data protection legislation and the inherent issues surrounding American companies holding records on the online activities of hundreds of millions of European citizens. Until 2016, flows of personal data between the EU and US were governed by the Safe Harbor Principles that placed obligations on US companies to abide by some core principles of data protection. These were deemed insufficient in 2016 by the EU as the block moved to stricter rules. As a result, the EU–US Privacy Shield came into force in July 2016 and, as of November 2019, is still active. Approximately 5,000 US companies have signed up to the agreement which is monitored annually by the European Commission. It is not clear whether the EU–US Privacy Shield is sustainable as many campaigners in EU member states have called for tighter regulations.

Concerns about transnational flows of personal data extend beyond the EU and US. Some of the most widely used communication and social media apps were developed in China, initially for the domestic market, but some are now expanding overseas. The social media video sharing app TikTok is perhaps the most successful of these, in 2020 claiming more than 1 billion users. However, the popularity of these apps amongst teenagers has prompted investigations and fines in a number of countries. In the US, the Federal Trade Commission (FTC) fined Bytedance, TikTok's owner, $5.7 million in 2019 for illegally collecting personal information from children under 13 (Hern, 2019a). In the same year, the UK's information commissioner announced an investigation into how the company prioritises the safety of children on its social network.

As two mobile platforms, iOS and Android, dominate the smartphone industry we can expect to see more cases such as these. App developers can easily launch products that have a potential reach of billions of consumers with relatively little investment. This trend will be accelerated by the rise of cheap wearable electronic devices such as fitness trackers and smart watches that will collect and send data via phone apps to distributed servers connected via the internet. Legislators and regulatory bodies will find it increasingly difficult to monitor this activity as apps can gain mass popularity in record times. Within 18 months of its international launch TikTok had gained more than 1 billion users outside of China, showing how a viral marketing strategy combined with an appeal to younger users can build a global user base before regulators have it on their radar (Hamilton, 2019).

Limits of regulation

Of course, simply outlawing certain activities does not mean those activities will stop. Determined criminals will find ways to avoid detection or loopholes that can be exploited while some will be caught but continue with their behaviour once their sentence is spent. Data regulations are no different, with companies exploiting geographic boundaries, under-resourced regulators and technical wizardry to bypass both the spirit and the letter of the law. Before its insolvency in 2018, Cambridge Analytica exploited the lax rules on the Facebook platform for gathering data from unwitting users to target niche groups of voters in the US and UK. While these rules have been tightened up in the interim, this example demonstrates the ease with which determined and skilled data marketers can hoover up the personal details of millions of individuals without consent being given.

In the 1980s and 1990s, most concerns over the collection and misuse of personal data centred on the activities of the state. The notion of an all-seeing 'Big Brother' using new surveillance technologies to monitor the movements and behaviour of citizens took inspiration from George Orwell's *1984* and Jeremy Bentham's designs for panoptic prisons (De Saulles and Horner, 2011; Foucault, 1977). The rapid growth of CCTV cameras in public spaces, particularly in the UK, in the 1990s accelerated the belief of many that privacy from an intruding state would soon be impossible. However, the rise of personal computing, the internet and, more recently, mobile computing has shifted much of the focus from the public sector to the private. The needs of the marketing and financial industries have driven demand for ever-increasing quantities of personal data to be collected as firms seek to reach ever-more precisely targeted groups (Campbell and Carlson, 2002; Gandy, 1993). In her detailed investigation and exposé of many of these activities, Zuboff (2019) refers to this phenomenon as Surveillance Capitalism. Zuboff draws parallels between the managerialism of Ford and General Motors in the twentieth century and the activities of Google and Facebook in the twenty-first. She fears that what begins as attempts by these internet giants to predict human behaviour so that profitable marketing messages can be placed in front of the relevant people is leading to a form of control as digital services become embedded in our daily lives both at home and work. Unlike many activities of the state, she argues, much of this activity remains either unregulated or beyond the understanding and control of regulatory bodies. As these companies move beyond their initial focus of helping us find information on the Web, communicate with friends or more conveniently buy goods online, Zuboff sees the entrenchment of surveillance by new methods.

> If Google is a search company, why it is investing in smart-home devices, wearables and self-driving cars? If Facebook is a social network, why is it developing drones and augmented reality? … In fact, activities that appear to be varied and even scattershot across a random selection of industries and projects are actually all the same activity guided by the same aim: behavioural surplus capture.
>
> *(Zuboff, 2019, p. 129)*

It is unlikely that the clock can be turned back and for these data giants to wind up their operations, or even be shut down by regulators. If this is a problem in need of a solution then more realistic approaches may be needed that redress the power balance between data subjects and data collectors. Data has the potential to solve

66 Challenges for policy and law makers

many of the world's problems if managed within a framework that balances the broader needs of society with the financial incentives of the marketplace. Opening up access to public and private datasets may be an important part of the solution but the dangers illustrated by the Cambridge Analytica scandal show the potential for things to go wrong. Tennison (2019) suggests that new institutions may be needed to manage this transition where data could be exchanged within a group of organisations for mutual benefit. She calls these data trusts, with the control over what can be shared overseen by an independent third party. This, she believes, could unlock the potential of public open data resources by providing a 'safe' environment for analysis and reuse. For example:

> gig economy workers might increase their negotiating power by giving them information about working conditions. Patient-led data trusts could help people with rare health conditions to donate records for research.
>
> *(Tennison, 2019)*

She acknowledges that there is still a lot of work to be done in this area but it offers a basis for rethinking how data could be used as a national resource rather than just as fuel for business models.

Before we reach the rise of data trusts, it is important that deficiencies in the current system are addressed. While data protection regulations in many countries provide citizens with the right to know what personal information is held on them by organisations, the practical task of accessing that information may not be simple. Part of the problem relates to the data sharing that goes on between organisations which consumers may not be aware of. The digital marketing industry relies on data sharing between a plethora of data brokers that collect data from our online activities and then sell it on to third parties that wish to use it for targeting their own markets. Thanks to a 2019 law in the US state of Vermont that requires companies buying and selling third-party personal data to register with the secretary of state, journalists Melendez and Pasternack (2019) identified 121 data brokers operating in the US. On one level this shows the law, intended to increase transparency in the data broking business, is working; however, as Melendez and Pasternack demonstrate, taking the next step of finding out what personal data these companies hold is more complex. While the Vermont law does not require brokers to give consumers access to their own data it does compel them to provide information about their opt-out systems – assuming, as the two authors state, they provide one. The process for opting out of having your data stored by any of the brokers relies on consumers contacting them individually and using whatever opt-out systems they may provide.

The New York Times journalist Kashmir Hill was surprised by the level of personal data held on her by consumer monitoring company Sift. Companies like Sift collect data on individual consumers from a variety of sources to create scores that can be used by third parties to determine, for example, how long someone can wait on hold when calling a business or whether we can return items to a store (Hill, 2019). Sift's proprietary scoring system relies on 16,000 factors that it tracks and 'judges whether or not you can be trusted, yet there is no file with your name that it can produce upon request' (Mims, 2019). By the end of 2019 and partly in response to public pressure, Sift did make individual files available and the results were interesting. Hill (2019) obtained hers, which ran to over 400 pages. She was surprised to find it included all the messages she had ever sent to hosts on Airbnb, several years of Yelp delivery orders as well as detailed information about how and when she had used her mobile phone. Hill argues that the opening up of this type of data by companies in the US is a response to the California Consumer Privacy Act that comes into force in the US in 2020. However, her experience is that just because a firm allows consumers to access this data it does not mean it is an easy process. The processes for doing this are often hidden in their privacy policies, she claims, and even when the company's procedures are followed it does not follow that the data will be released. Several companies she contacted either took weeks to respond or, in one case, never sent the report. US journalist Hu (2019) had a similar experience when she contacted five companies for her personal data and found long delays and requests for additional personal information to be common.

Another problem facing regulators is the changing nature of digital businesses and the impact this has on competition and market forces. The economics of a digital business that relies on the collection and trading of data differ to that of a more traditional industrial organisation. Regulation of firms in the industrial age often centred on the abuses of monopolies and duopolies in terms of their pricing. By definition, a market with little or no competition may allow dominant firms to charge excessive prices for their goods and services. This drove the breakup of Standard Oil in the US in 1911 and AT&T in 1984 where federal regulators believed more competition was needed via the creation of firms spun off from these giants. The extent to which this aim was achieved is debatable but the logic is compelling and success could be measured via falling prices for oil or telephone services. However, in digital markets where the end product or service is given away for free it is more difficult to argue that price gouging is taking place. Applying twentieth-century regulatory logic to these businesses would imply that Facebook or Google should be paying us to use their services. While that is a possibility it seems unlikely and so, perhaps, a different approach is needed.

Technology industry analyst Ben Thompson calls firms like Facebook and Google aggregators in that they aggregate the attention of consumers for the purposes of providing audiences for advertisers (Thompson, 2019). Aggregators are different, he argues, from platform operators such as Apple and Microsoft that operate platforms from which third parties can build profitable products and services. Regulatory approaches, he believes, need to be different for platform operators and aggregators as the ways in which they dominate their markets are different. Aggregators rely on the collection of consumer data at scale and their power comes from controlling demand. In this sense, he argues, regulators should focus more on the buying up of other aggregators by Facebook and Google as that can cement their market dominance by closing down competition before it can take hold. Facebook offers a good example of this through its acquisition of WhatsApp and Instagram, which could have become serious competitors had they remained independent. Whether forcing Facebook to sell off those two companies is viable is debatable but, if Thompson is to be believed, looking closely at what it and Google may acquire in the future is something to be taken seriously.

Finally, another problem faced by regulators in controlling the activities of data-driven firms is the frequent mismatch between requirements for making data anonymous and the reality of how easy it often is to deanonymise it. This was touched on earlier in the chapter but it highlights a problem with vast increases in the quantity of personal data and the power of information processing tools to understand links between seemingly disparate data points. Data anonymity has been a cornerstone of much medical and social research since the 1980s when large datasets started to become available. Many of the widely used anonymisation techniques date back to this era, before details on individual's finances, health, shopping and browsing habits became so widely available via the data brokers discussed previously (Bushwick, 2019). In a recent study of supposedly anonymous datasets, the authors found that 99.98% of Americans could be accurately identified in any of the collections using 15 demographic attributes (Rocher et al., 2019). They conclude that 'even heavily sampled anonymized datasets are unlikely to satisfy the modern standards for anonymization set forth by the GDPR' (Rocher et al., 2019, p. 1). A solution, they suggest, is for data brokers to develop new techniques for anonymisation to bring the industry into line with modern requirements. Whether this will simply trigger an arms race with unscrupulous data operators finding new ways to deanonymise these assets is debatable but the evidence seems clear that 30-year-old approaches are no longer sufficient.

Notable recent cases

Reported data breaches have been increasing year on year largely due to the growing scale of global data collections, sophisticated hackers and often lax security protocols by data collectors. According to security analysts Risk Based Security, the first six months of 2019 saw more data leaks than the whole of 2018, exposing 4.1 billion personal records (Risk Based Security, 2019). In 2018, British Airways admitted hackers had accessed records on 500,000 customers while in July 2019 bank Capital One discovered a breach that compromised social security numbers, credit scores and credit card transactions of more than 100 million customers (Armerding, 2019). Many cases go unreported although failure to admit breaches of personal data can result in criminal proceedings in some countries and do massive damage to company reputations. Even admitting data failures can still lead to large fines from regulators. The GDPR allows for far larger financial penalties than previous legislation, with the UK's Information Commissioner having proposed a record fine of £183 million on British Airways for its breach which, the regulator claimed, was due to poor security systems at the airline.

Challenges for policy and law makers **69**

While most data thefts appear to be for financial gain, the case of Cambridge Analytica highlights the potential threat to democratic processes that can arise from data misuse. The company adopted many of the techniques used by marketers to profile, understand and then target relevant groups of consumers. In 2017, Richard Robinson, the vice-president of the firm's commercial arm, stated in a presentation that:

> Enabling somebody and encouraging somebody to go out to vote on a wet Wednesday morning is no different in my mind to persuading and encouraging somebody to move from one toothpaste brand to another ... [it is] about understanding what message is relevant to that person at that time when they are in that particular mindset.
>
> *(Tett, 2017)*

Much of the controversy surrounding Cambridge Analytica's techniques is not because they were illegal *per se*, but that their approach of micro-targeting groups of voters with highly transient, heavily biased messages is not in keeping with the spirit of political campaigning. Facebook was fined by the UK's Information Commissioner for allowing Cambridge Analytica's app to access 87 million of its users' profiles, although the £500,000 penalty is unlikely to seriously worry the firm. Tett (2018) draws parallels between this activity and the behaviour of many banks leading up to the 2008 financial crisis where shady dealings in credit derivatives almost brought about the collapse of the Western financial system. The ignorance of financial regulators and politicians as to what these banks were doing and, therefore, the lack of understanding of the risks involved allowed their activities to go unchecked. The Cambridge Analytica case demonstrates, Tett argues, that data scientists have gone under the radar and it is time for regulators to better understand the tools and techniques they are using.

While Cambridge Analytica filed for insolvency proceedings in 2018 and, therefore, ceased operations, the repercussions of its actions carried on. The reputation of Facebook has been significantly tarnished with calls from across the political spectrum and in the media for the company to be investigated fully for its role, however unwitting. For advocates of greater transparency and accountability in the use of personal data, the Cambridge Analytica case can be seen as a positive development in that it brought to mainstream attention some of what goes on in the data shadows. It has started a debate that is leading to many questions being raised about how far we should let technology companies and those that employ them go in collecting and using personal information.

As equally sensitive as political manipulation via data misuse is the sharing of health-related information. Data on the lifestyle and health of individuals is particularly valuable to a range of stakeholders and presents difficult challenges for policymakers and regulators as they try to balance the broader needs of society with the protection of personal privacy. The mass collection and analysis of personal health data offers the potential for groundbreaking research in understanding and

70 Challenges for policy and law makers

finding cures for many diseases and conditions. In 2018, the UK's Department of Health and Social Care released a policy paper outlining the government's enthusiasm for using data more effectively to improve healthcare treatments and aid medical research.

> The potential of cutting-edge technologies to support preventative, predictive and personalised care is huge. For example, we could use more data-driven technologies such as artificial intelligence (AI) to help diagnose diseases or conditions and to gain better insights into treatments and preventions that could benefit all of society ... Open standards, secure identity and interoperability are critical to the safe and successful use of technology, ensuring that systems talk to each other and that the right data gets to the right place at the right time.
>
> *(Department of Health and Social Care, 2018)*

Based on the plethora of public-sector IT initiatives that ended in overspending and under-delivering, government claims about how new technologies will transform the delivery of public services need to be taken with a pinch of salt. The UK's Department of Health has a particularly bad reputation in this respect, having spent billions of pounds in the 2000s on its National Programme for IT that largely failed to live up to the hype of a digitally connected healthcare system (Collins, 2006; Maughan, 2010). However, most public-sector IT projects of the last 30 years have centred on streamlining back-office systems and improving workflows through the application of computerised systems. This reflects the investments made by much of the private sector over the same period resulting in the digitisation of previously analogue systems. More recently, many IT initiatives have focused on using data to improve operating efficiencies as well as to drive innovation and product development. In the NHS this is playing out in projects to harness the wealth of patient data to better understand causes of disease and potential cures. Both Google and Amazon have been involved in such projects with their expertise in handling data at scale as well as offering new ways to capture lifestyle data being seen by some policymakers in the NHS as being complementary to the aims of the health service. The UK is unusual in having a unified national system for the delivery of healthcare services that is freely accessible to all citizens at the point of delivery. This offers a uniquely large pool of health and patient data not available in most other countries where health services are spread across multiple companies, agencies and healthcare providers.

Google's first major project with the NHS started in late 2015 with an arrangement between the Royal Free Hospital in London and the company's artificial intelligence subsidiary, DeepMind. Under the deal, more than 1 million patient records were shared with DeepMind, which was contracted to build an app which would alert doctors about patients at risk of acute kidney injury (AKI) (Wakefield, 2017). When the deal became public in 2016, many commentators were concerned about the lack of consultation leading up to the arrangement and the

Challenges for policy and law makers **71**

particularly sensitive nature of the data being shared with a commercial company that had no track record of working in this sector. There were also criticisms that the hospital had not secured explicit consent from patients before sharing this data. These concerns resulted in an investigation by the Information Commissioner's Office and their findings in 2017 confirmed that proper procedures compliant with data protection legislation were not followed. In her summary of the findings, the Information Commissioner stated:

> There's no doubt the huge potential that creative use of data could have on patient care and clinical improvements, but the price of innovation does not need to be the erosion of fundamental privacy rights. Our investigation found a number of shortcomings in the way patient records were shared for this trial. Patients would not have reasonably expected their information to have been used in this way, and the Trust could and should have been far more transparent with patients as to what was happening.
>
> *(ICO, 2017)*

A further investigation by the ICO to check that DeepMind and the Royal Free had changed their working practices in the context of this deal found that the way data was being used by the Streams app was within the legal constraints set out in the GDPR (ICO, 2019).

While this case highlights the need for public bodies and the private firms they share data with to work within the framework of data protection and privacy legislation, it also raises a broader concern about the extent to which large technology companies should be involved with sensitive public data. Powles and Hodson (2017) argue that the DeepMind/Royal Free deal is worrying because it risks extending the massive power that Google has in the digital advertising sector to the healthcare space. Giving Google or other technology giants such as Apple, Amazon or Microsoft access to such important and sensitive data risks shutting out smaller competitors from developing and building apps and tools that could offer better solutions to the needs of the health service. The authors cite evidence of smaller AI companies declining to participate in markets where DeepMind has already made inroads. The deep pockets of Google to fund the company and employ leading researchers make it extremely difficult for competitors to develop rival products. Allowing the company to be the first to have access to this data and build AI algorithms around it risks that DeepMind will 'build, own and control networks of knowledge about disease' (Powles and Hodson, 2017, p. 364).

These fears may be given fresh impetus by more recent examples of links between the NHS and the technology sector. In 2019 the UK health secretary announced a partnership between the NHS and Amazon whereby the Alexa voice assistant would offer expert health advice to users that would reduce pressure on 'our hard-working GPs and pharmacists' (Walker, 2019). While this deal only allows the company access to health advice already published on the NHS website, campaigners have said it raises questions about transparency and could be seen as the thin end

72 Challenges for policy and law makers

of the wedge of public/private partnerships in this space. A copy of the legal contract between Amazon and the Secretary of State for Health and Social Care was obtained by the campaigning group Privacy International under the UK's Freedom of Information Act. Redacted sections on possible penalties for Amazon should it fail to honour the agreement highlight, according to Privacy International, a lack of transparency. Although permitted under the exemption of 'confidential sensitivity', the organisation claims is demonstrates that 'Amazon's commercial interest is superseding public interest' (Privacy International, 2019). It should be noted that the API from the NHS website that feeds the Alexa service is also used by more than 1,500 other organisations that integrate this data into their own services and applications (NHS Digital, 2019).

NHS Digital, which manages these arrangements, sees the technology as an important part of its health delivery service, particularly in a world that increasingly relies on voice assistants to find information. There is a strong argument that the health service should focus on delivering healthcare to its users and leave technical innovation to companies that are better equipped and financed to do so. However, the commercial pressures placed on private firms to always be growing and finding new revenue sources is central to the arguments of many critics of increased sharing of public data assets. An investigation by the *Financial Times* revealed the extent to which sensitive health data was being shared by some of the UK's most popular health websites with data brokers and advertising platforms including Google and Facebook and Amazon (Murgia and Harlow, 2019). Data included medical symptons, drug names, diagnoses and menstrual and fertility information. While this does not include the direct sharing of any NHS data, it raises the possibility of such data leaking into the large pools of health-related data being amassed by data brokers and advertising platforms. The relative ease with which 'anonymous' data can be deanonymised, discussed previously, presents a number of scenarios where personal searches for health-related questions could be linked to individual patient records. Although hypothetical at this stage, safeguards need to be put in place now to prevent such incidents before they can occur.

Having considered some recent cases of data misuse, the next section examines some of the rulings and proposals put forward for reform by policymakers and regulators.

Recent rulings and proposals

It is clear that data fuels much of the modern world in terms of innovation and economic growth. It has moved from being used to measure what was happening in industrial economies to becoming a resource in its own right. The last 20 years have seen some of the world's largest companies, new sectors and new rules of competition being created (*The Economist*, 2017). As data becomes a key resource and generator of wealth we have also seen it being misused as companies find ever more creative ways to circumvent the accepted rules of business and politics.

In 2019 the UK's Information Commissioner found that the adtech industry, dominated by Google and Facebook, was operating illegally (Murgia, 2019). At the heart of this lies the real-time bidding for ad space on websites where personal data is often used without consent. The lack of transparency in how the ad exchanges operate makes it almost impossible for anyone outside these companies to know where data is coming from and how it is being used. The Commissioner's report outlined how particularly sensitive data relating to a person's race, sexuality or political opinions was often a part of this data bartering and that security measures to protect anonymity were frequently lax. Similar investigations and reports have been produced in other countries where, although data protection rules may vary, there is a common concern that data trading is taking place beyond the gaze or control of regulators. The Australian Competition and Consumer Commission (ACCC) reported in 2019 on the rise of digital platforms and concluded that the market power of giants such as Google and Facebook and their growing share of advertising budgets was undermining the ability of traditional media outlets to remain profitable (ACCC, 2019). Like the UK's Information Commissioner, the ACCC was also concerned that several large internet companies were developing a stranglehold on the collection and management of consumer data, preventing new entrants from building sustainable business models. While the Commission acknowledged that consumers benefited from the 'free' services offered by Google, Facebook and others, too many users were not sufficiently aware of the data they were giving away or how it was being used behind the scenes.

Breaches of data protection and privacy rules are usually settled with fines and rulings that the offending behaviour must stop. In Europe the GDPR has seen a large increase in the potential fines that regulators can levy and several of the cases already discussed demonstrate they are not reluctant to do so. Legal prosecutions, large fines and the adverse publicity that goes with them are certainly a deterrent for many firms. However, there is a growing consensus that strict enforcement of ever-more stringent legislation may not be the only answer to the privacy concerns surrounding data misuse. Perhaps, it is argued, new ways of thinking about personal data are needed as well as new business models to reconfigure how data is collected, traded and used.

At the core of many of these potential approaches is a belief that personal data ownership is required if the balance between the commercial needs of business and the privacy demands of consumers is to be redressed. The argument runs that:

> data should be treated like property – something people can rent out or sell for fair compensation. As one example goes, you should own your data like you own a vehicle: if someone took your car and rented it out for others' benefit, you would care.
>
> *(Goldsmith, 2019)*

The intangible nature of data makes it difficult for many people to appreciate the value it holds and although most consumers would probably agree that protecting

74 Challenges for policy and law makers

personal privacy is important, the evidence is that most of us are not prepared to take steps to do so. This dichotomy is often referred to as the 'privacy paradox' and is more due to a lack of knowledge on the part of consumers than laziness (Kamleitner and Mitchell, 2019). As the systems developed by internet platforms and adtech businesses to capture and exploit data grown in sophistication, it is not surprising that end users struggle to know what steps to take to protect their privacy. The personal use of adblockers when browsing the Web is widespread but is not sufficient to prevent personal data leaking into the hands of data brokers and ad platforms. Many ad-supported sites will not display content if they detect an adblocker is being used and social media platforms cannot function without the exchange of data between and amongst users and the network owners.

In theory, empowering consumers to take control of their own data and letting them decide who has access to it and what firms should pay for the right to use it has a certain appeal. Many of the internet giants have built their business models and wealth on the free use of our data so demanding they start to pay us to continue doing so does not seem unreasonable. However, the practicalities of building systems that would make this possible are not necessarily simple. Any system would need to be simple enough for non-technical consumers to easily use, be robust in its security protocols and have a reliable system for tracking data exchanges and use as well as provide financial rewards for data owners.

Commercial data exchanges such as Terbine and Dawex offer solutions for large-scale data producers to buy and sell data but doing so at the individual level is more complex due to issues of scale and relatively low values for data transactions. It is possible that blockchain technologies could provide part of the solution as their distributed architecture provides a potentially more cost-effective way of authenticating transactions as well as being less susceptible to fraud and hacking. US company Algebraix Data believes its blockchain-based platform could be part of the solution which it claims will be able to handle hundreds of millions, possibly even billions, of users and manage their personal data transactions (Woodie, 2017). Whether this and other similar technologies are viable at this scale is less debatable than whether there is a public appetite to engage with such platforms. According to Algebraix Data's founder, participants could earn up to $2,000 per year through selling their data which, if true, could be a viable incentive for users to sign up. What the ad-supported companies like Google and Facebook would make of this is not clear.

However, whatever solutions may successfully come to market, there is evidence of a growing interest amongst policymakers in seeing the markets for personal data change. This might involve empowering consumers to take more control over their data but it could also focus on forcing the giants to open up their data to smaller competitors. While a handful of companies, so the argument goes, control most online activity and data monetisation, it is becoming increasingly difficult for new entrants to build successful data-driven business models. In 2018, the UK government announced a review into the 'emergence of powerful new companies' in the tech sector (Ram, 2018). Reporting in 2019, the review panel concluded that technology giants including Facebook, Google, Apple, Microsoft and Amazon were using their market dominance in digital services and data capture to unfairly boost their profits (Ram and Giles, 2019). The solution, it argued, would involve forcing these companies to open up their data for others to use. This stems from what the report authors called 'tipping', whereby once a company reaches a certain scale, often driven by network effects or externalities, a tipping can occur which allows the winner to take most of a market. This has certainly been the case in search with Google and social networking with Facebook. Opening up the data assets of some of these dominant players and, thus, creating more competitive markets could be an effective addition to existing data protection legislation. Like previous discussions of freeing up personal data, however, the report emphasises the need for personal data mobility but is rather vague on details as to how this might be enabled.

Perhaps not coincidentally, some of the larger technology companies have responded with proposals and ideas of their own for ways consumers can be better protected and how the markets in which they operate become more competitive. This is a difficult balancing act for these firms as they are under pressure from the financial markets to consistently increase profits and market share. Their increasingly sophisticated new products and services also rely on new ways to capture and use personal data. The voice assistants offered by Google, Amazon and Apple are good examples of how these companies are finding new ways for consumers to interact with their digital platforms and, as a consequence, give away even more data. At its annual conference for developers in 2019, Google exemplified this quandary as it announced a new version of its digital assistant, which could construct a 'graph' of a user's interests and preferences and a 'smart screen' for households that is fitted with cameras that can recognise users (Waters, 2019). At the same event the company also revealed new settings that its customers could access to instruct Google how long the company could keep records of their online activities as well as providing new tools for anonymous surfing. However, critics were quick to respond that these changes were too little, too late. The director of the US Center for Digital Democracy stated:

> This is a drop in the digital bucket. It would take a wholesale reinvention, along with Facebook, of how they make money to make a real difference.
>
> *(Waters, 2019)*

New regulatory approaches and stricter legal regimes seem highly likely over the coming years. The speed of growth and scale of some of the largest digital platforms has caught policymakers and regulators by surprise. International cultural differences and the geographic roots of technology companies are playing a part in some of the proposed solutions but, as this section has alluded to, perhaps some more creative ways of thinking about the problems are required. The next section explores some of the discussions in more detail about future regulatory approaches.

76 Challenges for policy and law makers

The future of data regulation

As data becomes an ever-more important input to developed economies and new technologies and services capture new sources, it is inevitable that new regulatory approaches will be needed. Just as the rise of new forms of banking and financial services since the 1980s have led to the creation of new regulatory bodies and rules, so the data revolution will require the same. Financial services regulators were caught out by the ingenuity of bankers as they found ways to circumvent existing rules to create new financial instruments that were misunderstood by the institutions tasked with overseeing the industry. Computing technologies played an important part in this revolution as data could be distributed and analysed far more quickly than previously and allowed analysts and traders to move into new sectors, leading to the rise of hedge funds that could place bets on almost any event that had a degree of uncertainty about it. Whether financial regulators have caught up with the activities of hedge funds and investment banks is highly debatable. The financial crash of 2008 certainly demonstrated that constant vigilance and oversight would be required if a repeat of the disaster was to be avoided in the future.

The future of data regulation is, arguably, more complicated than that required for the financial sector. The Internet Revolution has transformed the structures of a number of industries and, as a consequence, their value chains. This is largely due to the nature of digitised information and how it can be created, distributed and consumed differently to its analogue cousin. Where the marginal costs of data distribution are near-zero and consumers have access to networks and devices that can bring that data to them wherever they are, it is inevitable that legacy supply and value chains will be disrupted. This is especially true in the case of journalism and the media sector. While the cost of creating original news and entertainment content remains the same, distribution by the internet to apps and smart end devices has dramatically fallen in price and, as a consequence, allowed new entrants into the market. Technology companies such as Google, Amazon and Apple have set up media creation and distribution divisions while new companies such as Netflix, Now TV (owned by Sky) and Hulu (owned by Disney) act as aggregators for content creators. At the same time, the commodification of news content has put pressure on traditional newspaper publishers to adapt their business models to a digital world. The over-arching challenge for all incumbent media firms is to find new ways to fund their operations as the traditional gatekeepers of content distribution give way to new models in reconfigured value chains.

In their study of the phenomenon of 'fake news' and the challenges that traditional publishers face in dealing with news distributed over social networks, Braun and Eklund (2019) argue that the:

> traditional subsidies provided to news organisations by advertisers have begun to collapse as more and more media consumption has migrated to the internet.
>
> *(Braun and Eklund, 2019, p. 2)*

This is leading, they claim, to an environment where the democratic role of journalism in exposing the 'truth' of events within the political and economic spheres is becoming incompatible with the rise of programmatic advertising discussed previously. Part of the solution may be for established news outlets to work as data brokers more than creators of news content to help consumers navigate the plethora of content pushed at them every day. From a policy and legal perspective, this could require new organisations to move to non-profit status with a public funding model, 'perhaps underwritten by a trust to which the largest ad tech players must contribute a portion of their revenues' (Braun and Eklund, 2019, p. 18).

In the short term, this seems an unlikely development as it would require a significant change of thinking by both news outlets and the public bodies responsible for regulating them. However, it is an idea worth considering as it highlights the need to examine what goes on in the background of the news and advertising sectors rather than just at the consumption end. Consumers are largely unaware of the systems being used to deliver their social media news feeds or the funding models behind them and a programme of education may be part of the solution.

Nadler et al. (2018) take this argument further and suggest that the infrastructure of data collection and consumer targeting used by the advertising sector is creating dangerous opportunities for political manipulation and other anti-democratic activities. They call this the 'Digital Influence Machine' (DIM) and claim it is a form of weaponisation for targeting vulnerable groups and individuals. This goes far beyond traditional critiques of the advertising industry that see it as a sophisticated system for persuading consumers to buy products and services they often do not need. The digitisation of the tools and techniques to allow micro-targeting has, they argue, politicised what was a largely benign sector. Nadler et al. focus on activities in the US and see the EU's GDPR as a useful framework which should be considered as it offers a right-based approach to data protection where consumers are given higher priority than in their own country. They propose tighter regulations on how social platforms carry political advertising, making them more transparent about which groups and individuals are funding messages. Since the 2016 US presidential election, public pressure on disclosing such information has resulted in Facebook amending its policy on political advertising. Going even further, Twitter announced in 2019 it was banning all political ads on its network. While some commentators welcomed this move and argued that Facebook should follow suit, others have claimed a side-effect will be to make it more difficult for smaller groups to spread their messages with larger, established political organisations benefiting the most due to the cost-efficient nature of advertising on social networks (McGregor, 2019).

Perhaps part of the problem in creating appropriate regulatory environments for legislating on the uses of personal data rests with the responsive nature of those charged with drafting it. This is largely inevitable as regulators must respond to events and advances in technology and the ways it is used. However, it can be argued that these bodies and policymakers need to take a step back and devise legislation from a more informed position. There is a danger that regulators see 'the internet' as a single entity rather than a complex system of interconnected networks, technologies and

78 Challenges for policy and law makers

businesses. As discussed in an earlier section of this chapter, Thompson (2019) argues that policymakers need to understand the differences between platform operators and aggregators if they are to design effective legislation. In Thompson's model, Google's search business is an aggregator as it acts as an intermediary between users and third-party content creators, while Windows, iOS and Android are platforms as they offer an ecosystem for third parties to build applications on. These differences confer different power to their operators with platforms generally able to lock users and developers more firmly into their environments. While Google search is dominant in its market, using another search engine such as Microsoft's Bing is only a click away. Google maintains it dominance by offering a preferred service for users in terms of results and has also been able to integrate it into the Android mobile operating system. Moving from iOS to Android or vice versa, on the other hand, is not impossible but requires users to change handsets, applications and learn how to use a different system. Deciding how and where to regulate these services requires an understanding of the technology stacks underpinning them and knowing where they are situated. Operating systems are further down the stack as they form the platform from which services such as web searching can take place.

This understanding leads to questions about what exactly legislators are trying to regulate for. Is it to enforce greater competition to allow new entrants into a market, is it to protect personal data or is it to prevent the spread of misinformation? Overarching all these questions is the issue of geographic boundaries and transnational data flows. Cultural differences and differing political regimes make it unlikely that global rules can be established to cover these issues in the way that trade agreements have opened up the distribution of products and services between many nations. The views of Chinese leaders on the role of the state in setting rules for data sharing are clearly different to those in much of Europe and this is unlikely to change in the near future. The escalation of a trade war between the US and China illustrates how quickly international disputes can form.

These differences are, perhaps, best illustrated by recent developments in the 'net neutrality' debates and the very different legislation being implemented in the US and Europe. Net neutrality refers to the practice in many countries of treating the provision of internet connectivity as a public utility with internet traffic being treated equally by carriers regardless of its source, the information it carries or the devices it will be delivered to. This carries on the tradition of most telecommunication providers in their provision of telephone services to consumers where, for most of the twentieth century, they were run by government bodies and offered standardised and regulated voice services. In the US, this is referred to as a Title II common carrier service and, until 2018, the rules for common carriers were applied to the delivery of internet services. However, the election of Donald Trump as president in 2016 and his appointment of a new head of the regulatory body, the FCC, has seen that policy change. Since June 2018, internet service providers (ISPs) have been reclassified in the US as Title I information services, which frees them of this obligation to provide equal carriage to all types of internet data (Shepardson, 2018). Under Title I rules, ISPs must inform consumers if they are blocking or slowing content or offering paid 'fast lanes' to content owners and application developers. This potentially threatens the internet ecosystem of services and applications that has thrived on an open internet that has created a hotbed of innovations from start-ups and, in 20 years, changed how billions of consumers communicate, find and share information, entertain themselves and access retail and financial services. Critics from a range of industries as well as policymakers and regulators were quick to argue against the FCC's change of classification, with the acting New York Attorney General Barbara Underwood stating:

> the repeal of net neutrality would allow internet service providers to put their profits before the consumers they serve and control what we see, do, and say online.
>
> *(Shepardson, 2018)*

In Europe, the principles of net neutrality have been more firmly upheld, with EU regulations providing a framework for member states to enforce equal access and carriage of data. Critics point to potential loopholes in EU rules that allow some mobile providers to offer consumers access to popular services such as Facebook and WhatsApp without incurring data charges, often referred to as 'zero-rating'. While this may not be strictly outside the law, it is often argued that zero-rating undermines the spirit of net neutrality in that it favours some services over others.

It is possible that the divergence of regulations in Europe and the US with respect to net neutrality as well as different approaches in other countries will see a fragmentation of the internet as we have known it. The ability of consumers to take for granted that they will be able to access any 'legal' services via their internet connections may no longer be the case for hundreds of millions of them. This could have considerable knock-on effects for innovation and the development of new services and applications. If the student founders of Google and Facebook had been obliged to outbid established competitors with deeper pockets for access to the internet then it is less likely they would have succeeded. It has been the open nature of the internet and the level playing field that provides for new entrants that has been one of the major factors for its widespread adoption. Turning back the clock now to an age of telecommunications providers acting as arbiters of what we can do online would have a negative impact on future digital innovations and services.

The next section looks forward to a world where computing and communication devices are embedded in our home and work lives and where the data flowing from these systems is set to transform societies at every level.

References

ACCC (2019). *Digital Platforms Enquiry – Final Report* (p. 42). Australian Competition and Consumer Commission.

Angwin, J. (2010, July 31). The Web's New Gold Mine: Your Secrets. *The Wall Street Journal.* www.wsj.com/articles/SB10001424052748703940904575395073512989404.

80 Challenges for policy and law makers

Armerding, T. (2019, December 10). Cost of Data Breaches in 2019: The 4 Worst Hits on the Corporate Wallet. Security Boulevard. https://securityboulevard.com/2019/12/cost-of-data-breaches-in-2019-the-4-worst-hits-on-the-corporate-wallet/.

Braun, J.A. & Eklund, J.L. (2019). Fake News, Real Money: Ad Tech Platforms, Profit-Driven Hoaxes, and the Business of Journalism. *Digital Journalism*, 7(1), 1–21.

Bushwick, S. (2019, July 23). 'Anonymous' Data Won't Protect Your Identity. Scientific American. www.scientificamerican.com/article/anonymous-data-wont-protect-your-identity/.

Campbell, J.E. & Carlson, M. (2002). Panopticon.com: Online Surveillance and the Commodification of Privacy. *Journal of Broadcasting & Electronic Media*, 46(4), 586–606.

Collins, T. (2006, October 29). Government IT: What Happened to our £25bn? *Computer Weekly*. www.computerweekly.com/news/2240103683/Government-IT-What-happened-to-our-25bn.

De Saulles, M. & Horner, D.S. (2011). The Portable Panopticon: Morality and Mobile Technologies. *Journal of Information, Communication and Ethics in Society*, 9(3), 206–216.

Department of Health and Social Care (2018, October 17). The Future of Healthcare: Our Vision for Digital, Data and Technology in Health and Care. GOV.UK. www.gov.uk/government/publications/the-future-of-healthcare-our-vision-for-digital-data-and-technology-in-health-and-care/the-future-of-healthcare-our-vision-for-digital-data-and-technology-in-health-and-care.

European Commission (2019, July 18). European Legislation on Open Data and the Re-Use of Public Sector Information [Text]. Digital Single Market. https://ec.europa.eu/digital-single-market/en/european-legislation-reuse-public-sector-information.

Foucault, M. (1977). *Discipline and Punish: The Birth of the Prison*. Random House.

FTC (2014). Data Brokers: A Call For Transparency and Accountability: A Report of the Federal Trade Commission (May 2014). Federal Trade Commission. www.ftc.gov/reports/data-brokers-call-transparency-accountability-report-federal-trade-commission-may-2014.

Gandy, O. (1993). The Panoptic Sort: A Political Economy of Personal Information. Critical Studies in Communication and in the Cultural Industries. University of Minnesota Press.

Goldsmith, C. (2019, March 18). Nothing Personal: The Importance of Creating Data Ownership Frameworks. European CEO. www.europeanceo.com/industry-outlook/nothing-personal-the-importance-of-creating-data-ownership-frameworks/.

Hamilton, I.A. (2019, November 18). TikTok Hit 1.5 Billion Downloads, and is Still Outperforming Instagram. *Business Insider*. www.businessinsider.com/tiktok-hits-15-billion-downloads-outperforming-instagram-2019-11.

Hern, A. (2019a, July 2). TikTok Under Investigation over Child Data Use. *The Guardian*. www.theguardian.com/technology/2019/jul/02/tiktok-under-investigation-over-child-data-use.

Hern, A. (2019b, July 23). 'Anonymised' Data Can Never be Totally Anonymous, Says Study. *The Guardian*. www.theguardian.com/technology/2019/jul/23/anonymised-data-never-be-anonymous-enough-study-finds.

Hill, K. (2019, November 4). I Got Access to My Secret Consumer Score. Now You Can Get Yours, Too. *The New York Times*. www.nytimes.com/2019/11/04/business/secret-consumer-score-access.html.

Hu, J. (2019, November 11). What Do You Know About Me? Slate. https://slate.com/technology/2019/11/sift-retail-equation-request-data-consumer-trustworthiness.html.

ICO (2017, July 3). Royal Free – Google DeepMind Trial Failed to Comply with Data Protection Law. Information Commissioner's Office. https://ico.org.uk/about-the-ico/news-and-events/news-and-blogs/2017/07/royal-free-google-deepmind-trial-failed-to-comply-with-data-protection-law/.

ICO (2019, July 31). Royal Free NHS Foundation Trust update, July 2019. Information Commissioner's Office. https://ico.org.uk/about-the-ico/news-and-events/news-and-blogs/2019/07/royal-free-nhs-foundation-trust-update-july-2019/.

Kamleitner, B. & Mitchell, V. (2019). Your Data Is My Data: A Framework for Addressing Interdependent Privacy Infringements. *Journal of Public Policy & Marketing, 38*(4), 433–450.

Maughan, A. (2010, September 13). Six Reasons Why the NHS National Programme For IT Failed. *Computer Weekly.* www.computerweekly.com/opinion/Six-reasons-why-the-NHS-National-Programme-for-IT-failed.

McGregor, S.C. (2019, November 4). Why Twitter's Ban on Political Ads Isn't as Good as it Sounds. *The Guardian.* www.theguardian.com/commentisfree/2019/nov/04/twitters-political-ads-ban.

Melendez, S. & Pasternack, A. (2019, March 2). Here are the Data Brokers Quietly Buying and Selling Your Personal Information. Fast Company. www.fastcompany.com/90310803/here-are-the-data-brokers-quietly-buying-and-selling-your-personal-information.

Mims, C. (2019, April 6). The Secret Trust Scores Companies Use to Judge Us All. *The Wall Street Journal.* www.wsj.com/articles/the-secret-trust-scores-companies-use-to-judge-us-all-11554523206.

Murgia, M. (2019, June 20). Adtech Industry Operating Illegally, Rules UK Regulator. *Financial Times.* www.ft.com/content/0620c0e4-9351-11e9-aea1-2b1d33ac3271.

Murgia, M. & Harlow, M. (2019, November 13). How Top Health Websites are Sharing Sensitive Data with Advertisers. *Financial Times.* www.ft.com/content/0fbf4d8e-022b-11ea-be59-e49b2a136b8d.

Murgia, M. & Ram, A. (2019, January 8). Data Brokers: Regulators Try to Rein in the 'Privacy Deathstars'. *Financial Times.* www.ft.com/content/f1590694-fe68-11e8-aebf-99e208d3e521.

Nadler, A., Crain, M. & Donovan, J. (2018). Weaponizing the Digital Influence Machine. Data & Society Research Institute. https://datasociety.net/output/weaponizing-the-digital-influence-machine/.

NHS Digital (2019, July 25). How We Are Talking to Alexa. https://digital.nhs.uk/blog/transformation-blog/2019/how-we-are-talking-to-alexa.

Orna, E. (2008). Information Policies: Yesterday, Today, Tomorrow. *Journal of Information Science, 34*(4), 547–565.

Powles, J. & Hodson, H. (2017). Google DeepMind and Healthcare in an Age of Algorithms. *Health and Technology, 7*(4), 351–367

Privacy International (2019, December 6). Alexa, What is Hidden behind Your Contract with the NHS? http://privacyinternational.org/long-read/3298/alexa-what-hidden-behind-your-contract-nhs.

Ram, A. (2018, August 1). UK Appoints Former Obama Adviser to Lead Tech Review. *Financial Times.* www.ft.com/content/3352b782-9593-11e8-b67b-b8205561c3fe.

Ram, A. & Giles, C. (2019, March 13). Tech Giants Should 'Open Up their Customer Data to Others'. *Financial Times.* www.ft.com/content/4180f5e6-44b4-11e9-a965-23d669740bfb.

Risk Based Security (2019). 2019 Mid-Year Data Breach Report (Cyber Risk Analytics). https://pages.riskbasedsecurity.com/2019-midyear-data-breach-quickview-report.

Rocher, L., Hendrickx, J.M. & de Montjoye, Y.-A. (2019). Estimating the Success of Re-Identifications in Incomplete Datasets Using Generative Models. *Nature Communications*, *10*(1), 1–9.

Shepardson, D. (2018, May 10). U.S. 'Net Neutrality' Rules Will Expire on June 11: FCC. Reuters. www.reuters.com/article/us-usa-internet-idUSKBN1IB1UN.

Solove, D.J. (2016). *A Brief History of Information Privacy Law* (No. 215; GWU Law School Public Law Research Paper). GWU Law School. https://papers.ssrn.com/abstract=914271.

Standage, T. (1999). *The Victorian Internet* (new edn). W&N.

Tennison, J. (2019, April 28). New Institutions are Needed for the Digital Age. *Financial Times*. www.ft.com/content/5f46f102-6741-11e9-b809-6f0d2f5705f6.

Tett, G. (2017, September 29). Trump, Cambridge Analytica and How Big Data is Reshaping Politics. *Financial Times*. www.ft.com/content/e66232e4-a30e-11e7-9e4f-7f5e6a7c98a2.

Tett, G. (2018, July 12). The Cambridge Analytica Scandal Echoes the Financial Crisis. *Financial Times*. www.ft.com/content/b21ffb20-85b1-11e8-96dd-fa565ec55929.

The Economist (2017, May 6). Data is Giving Rise to a New Economy. www.economist.com/briefing/2017/05/06/data-is-giving-rise-to-a-new-economy.

Thompson, B. (2019, December 9). A Framework for Regulating Competition on the Internet. Stratechery. https://stratechery.com/2019/a-framework-for-regulating-competition-on-the-internet/.

Wakefield, J. (2017, March 17). Google DeepMind's NHS Deal under Scrutiny. BBC News. www.bbc.com/news/technology-39301901.

Walker, A. (2019, December 8). NHS Gives Amazon Free Use of Health Data under Alexa Advice Deal. *The Guardian*. www.theguardian.com/society/2019/dec/08/nhs-gives-amazon-free-use-of-health-data-under-alexa-advice-deal.

Waters, R. (2019, May 8). Google Promises to Give Users More Control of Data. *Financial Times*. www.ft.com/content/65a20d1c-7159-11e9-bf5c-6eeb837566c5.

Woodie, A. (2017, December 7). Blockchain At Heart of Personal Data Monetization Service. Datanami. www.datanami.com/2017/12/07/blockchain-heart-new-data-monetization-service/.

Zuboff, S. (2019). *The Age of Surveillance Capitalism: The Fight for a Human Future at the New Frontier of Power*. Profile Books.

6

PERVASIVE COMPUTING AND DATA FUTURES

Pervasive computing and the Internet of Things

The next, and most significant, phase in the data revolution is being driven by the installation of billions of low-cost computing devices in everyday places. This is often referred to as the Internet of Things (IoT) but has also been defined as ubiquitous or pervasive computing. The phrase IoT is attributed to Kevin Ashton who, as a brand manager for Proctor and Gamble in 1989, realised the potential for RFID tags to streamline the global supply chains his company were part of. RFID tags are tiny, very cheap, passive chips that can store and transmit digital information. They are used across a range of industries and for multiple purposes including the self-checking in and out of library books and by the retail sector to prevent shoplifting. Ashton saw how RFID tags could be applied to goods as they moved through the supply chain enabling factories, warehouses and retailers to track items as they passed in and out of their premises far more efficiently than the manual entering of information into systems by employees. Ashton's 1989 vision for an 'Internet of Things' is summarised by Kellmereit and Obodovski (2013).

> Information about objects – like Gillette razor blades or Pantene shampoo – would be stored on the internet, and the smart tag om the object would just point to this information.
>
> *(Kellmereit and Obodovski, 2013, p. 17)*

Looking back on his original vision ten years later, Ashton claims the key benefit of a fully formed IoT would be computers harvesting data from RFID and sensor-enabled objects automatically rather than relying on humans to input the information (Ashton, 2009). Computers, he argues, are far more efficient than people at collecting, managing and inputting data and that by taking humans out of the

84 Pervasive computing and data futures

equation we could be creating a new digital revolution more significant than that started by the internet.

It is worth noting that automated or mechanised systems for collecting data can be traced back to mid-nineteenth-century Russia, when a data transmission circuit was established between the tsar's Winter Palace and Russian army headquarters to exchange logistics information (Mayo-Wells, 1963). During the twentieth century, telemetry was widely used by power-generating plants to remotely monitor power outputs of power stations and loading on transmission networks. The first wireless telemetry systems were used in weather balloons and these were then installed in aircraft to monitor flight performance (Foster, 1965). The Second World War saw significant progress in wireless telemetry for aircraft as well as in the emerging rocket-based weapons developed in Germany. These technologies were adopted by the American space programme and were instrumental in getting men to the moon. Later in the twentieth century, these systems became more sophisticated, leading to the term 'machine-to-machine' (M2M) being used to describe a wide range of functions and networks that were being deployed across industrial sectors.

The IoT is a natural evolution of these trends as it brings together the emergence of low-cost computing components with the internet as a pervasive network for carrying data. While Ashton's original vision saw RFID tags as the core driver of an IoT, developments over the succeeding 30 years have realised a far more powerful and economically transforming system. A useful definition of this new interconnected environment is provided by industry analysts Gartner:

> The Internet of Things is the network of physical objects that contain embedded technology to communicate and sense or interact with their internal states or the external environment.
>
> *(Gartner, 2016)*

Investments by telecommunications and computing companies as well as adopting firms across a range of industries are making the IoT a rapidly growing and significant sector. IDC believes worldwide spending on the IoT reached $745 billion in 2019 and is forecast to grow to $1.2 trillion by 2022 (IDC, 2019a). In terms of actual devices, telecommunications equipment provider Ericsson estimates 10.8 billion at the end of 2019 and 24.9 billion by 2025 (Ericsson, 2019).

While this growth is impressive with respect to scale and value, it is important to remember that the core purpose of these IoT installations is to collect data. For the first 60 years of the Computing Revolution, most computing systems were designed to process data that already existed for the purposes of raising operational efficiencies within firms and to streamline the processes of the public sector. Mobile computing through the rise of smartphones saw the closer integration of digital technologies into our daily lives and environments. The IoT is capturing new forms of data from activities that have often remained outside the scope of automation. It is also speeding up and increasing the volumes of data available for processing and analysis by ever-more-powerful back-end systems.

The following sections explore how the IoT and associated technologies are being deployed across cities, workplaces, homes and on our bodies. The impact of AI and ML on data analysis is considered in the context of creating new opportunities for businesses as well as the challenges that may arise.

The IoT at work

Following the Industrial Revolutions brought about by the application of steam power in the eighteenth century and electricity and semiconductors in the twentieth, it has been claimed we are now entering a Fourth Industrial Revolution driven by a 'ubiquitous and mobile internet, by smaller and more powerful sensors that have become cheaper, and by artificial intelligence and machine learning' (Schwab, 2016, p. 7). The workplace is where we are seeing many of these investments take place as the drive for greater efficiencies and profit is forcing companies to adapt to a more digital world. Just as very few companies could afford to resist investing in computing infrastructure if they wished to remain competitive, so modern firms are having to adapt to the digital transformation of their operations often via the IoT. It has been estimated by consulting firm McKinsey and Co. that the successful digital transformation of the global industrial sector would be worth between $0.8 trillion and $2 trillion via revenue growth and efficiency gains (Atluri et al., 2018). McKinsey sees entire industries and their value chains being transformed through the application of digital technologies. A good example of a global industrial giant recognising this shift is General Electric (GE), which has emphasised that its over-arching strategy is to move from making 'things' to software via the embedding of intelligence into its products and the multi-billion-dollar investment in its industrial automation software platform Predix (Bloede, 2017).

Other firms with an industrial heritage are also embracing digital platforms as they seek to remain relevant in a data-reliant world, including Siemens, Bosch and Hitachi. Siemens describes its Mindsphere platform as an 'open IT operating system that connects your products, plants, systems, and machines, enabling you to harness the wealth of data generated by the IoT with advanced analytics' (Siemens, 2019). Bosch's IoT suite of services is similar in that it offers customers the opportunity to analyse data generated by the firm's products and is seeing the company explore different pricing models based on data usage rather than simply the capital costs of equipment. The Hitachi Insight Group was established in 2016 as its IoT subsidiary and relies on its Lumada IoT platform to offer a suite of data capture and processing solutions (Ali, 2018).

These and other similar platforms offer useful starting points from which third parties and end users can build applications and services that use data to transform industrial processes and develop innovative products. Some of the most interesting applications are in industries where the Computing Revolution has traditionally had less impact. A raft of new products and services are being developed for the agriculture sector where the deployment of sensors on farms, animals and equipment is providing farmers with unprecedented volumes of data to improve their practices.

86 Pervasive computing and data futures

Agtech innovations are being driven by both the availability of cheaper sensors but also by the increasing demands placed on farmers by rising populations, climate change and the environmental degradation of much agricultural land from years of intensive farming. By 2050 it is predicted global food demand will increase by between 59% and 98% and water resources will become scarcer and healthy soil more difficult to maintain (Wholey, 2019). The rise of more connected farms that collect and harvest data as well as crops will help shift the balance of power in access to data that has typically been controlled by agricultural suppliers. An example is the Farmer's Business Network (FBN), which comprises 5,000 participating farms covering 16 million acres and allows farmers to anonymously share data about all their activities from seed performance to chemical pricing (Wholey, 2019). Farmobile represents the next generation of data collection and sharing, where its network of sensors covers more than 700 farms and collects data from fields and farm equipment. This data is used to benefit the farmer from whose land it is collected and is also available to buy for other farmers or interested third parties (Janzen, 2019). Being able to monitor and analyse real-time as well as historical data on field conditions and the state of crops combined with precision seed drilling and fertiliser spreading by smart tractors allows a far more efficient use of land and reduces the resources needed to attain successful harvests. In Taiwan, climate change is making it more difficult for farmers to predict weather patterns with severe weather events such as typhoons wiping out entire crops. The mass deployment of sensors in rice fields is helping farmers and the buyers of their crop monitor rain, temperature and chemicals in the soil as well as allowing them to optimise their production cycles in the face of unpredictable weather patterns (Hille, 2018).

Being able to better predict unusual events through the collection of sensor data is also attracting the attention of the insurance industry, where managing risk has always been a core part of the business. A good example of the type of company emerging to exploit the IoT in this sector is Corvus Insurance, which was set up in 2016 to collect data from more than 50 sources to help corporate clients in the food and pharmaceutical industries better predict and prevent losses (Loizos, 2018). The company uses IoT data from multiple types of sensors including those placed in rooves which can measure the pressure resulting from snow and predict the likelihood of a claim being made from a collapse.

While insurance companies can financially benefit from the IoT by the better management of risk, other sectors also stand to improve the safety of their employees by better understanding risk. The oil and gas industry has been using sensors distributed across its mining operations for a number of years but the recent rise of real-time monitoring and being able to process this data at speed and scale is having a significant impact. On a typical oil well, a driller may have up to 70 different companies' products in use but, until recently, these were all separately collecting data in formats and to systems that could not talk to each other (Gold, 2019). IoT-based systems such as that used by BP integrate these different data flows and allow a more comprehensive overview of operations that is better placed to predict problems before they arise. BP has been an innovator in the use of such systems since its 2010 Gulf of Mexico explosion and oil spill in which 11 people died and almost 5 million barrels of oil leaked into the ocean. In 2015, the company contracted GE and its Predix data gathering and analytics platform to connect 650 wells with up to 30 sensors each to measure oil pressure and temperature and other variables (Moon, 2015). The integration of these data sources into a unified view on the Predix platform for real-time analysis offers BP a more accurate and timely view of operations. It is anticipated this will increase the likelihood of potentially dangerous pressure build-ups being detected before they could lead to an explosion.

A common feature linking many of these IoT industrial deployments are the systems at the back end that are able to process captured data and produce actionable insights in near-real-time. Business reporting has traditionally been a rearview-mirror exercise where the insights were useful to help analysts understand why something happened but did not help them prevent it from happening in the first place. Platforms such as GE's Predix, fed with constantly updated data from sensors, are able to draw on massive computing power and apply machine learning (ML) techniques to large datasets. The results of this analysis can be fed back directly to those who need it only moments after the data is generated by the sensors. Ever-expanding historical datasets can also be used to train the systems and improve the ML algorithms.

There are two key impacts emerging from the IoT revolution that is taking place across many industries. The first is the potential for increased efficiencies and the radical restructuring of processes and workflows. This will provide greater profits for those firms able to harness these changes, and will put those that cannot out of business. For society at large, these efficiencies could help in the battle against climate change as fewer resources will be required to produce the same number of goods or services. The second impact will revolve around the access to and control of the data that is generated by the industrial IoT. The rise of distributed sensor networks within and across firms and industries has the potential to democratise data flows in that it may not be simply be the larger conglomerates that control it. Smaller producers have traditionally been at a disadvantage when it comes to having access to strategic data with only larger competitors having the scale to collect and manage it. Distributed networks such as Farmobile discussed above and similar ventures in other sectors could create a more level playing field with data exchanges and cooperative-style arrangements driving this change.

The IoT at home

The 'smart' or 'connected' home describes the implementation of IoT technologies in the domestic space. Pundits have been predicting the rise of the smart home since the 1950s when new electrical devices started to appear in the household but it is only in the last few years that truly smart and connected technologies have begun to proliferate around us. These include smart doorbells, lighting, speakers, thermostats and vacuum cleaners. The common feature of all these devices is their

88 Pervasive computing and data futures

ability to collect data and connect to the outside world via the internet. The global revenue of smart home hardware and associated services was estimated to be almost $120 billion in 2019, with major players including Google, Apple, Samsung and Amazon taking a large share of this (Wodark, 2017). Over the last decade, many start-ups have also been launched to build and market smart devices for the home with investment funding into these companies peaking at around $500 million in 2014 (CB Insights, 2015). Since then the market has matured somewhat with large technology firms buying some of the most successful ventures. From a consumer perspective, the key reasons for purchasing smart home devices are security monitoring, energy management, home automation and entertainment.

Some of the broad product groups and the companies producing products and services for them include the following.

> Smart speakers. These are the voice assistant devices that connect us to the digital ecosystems of some of the large technology companies. Amazon had the largest market share of this category in 2018 with 65% of all devices connecting to the Alexa platform, followed by Google (20%), Apple (5%) and other platforms taking 10% (Rao, 2019). While the platforms are dominated by the technology giants, it is important to note that a number of third-party developers are entering the voice assistant market with their own products that connect to the major platforms including Lenovo, Sonos and JBL. This is similar to the smartphone market, which until very recently offered competing operating systems, some of which were open to third-party developers and others that were more proprietary.
>
> Monitors. These typically use video cameras to record activities within households and may be embedded in doorbells or placed in rooms to keep an eye on children and babies. Google's Nest Cam with built-in camera can be used as a baby monitor while Amazon's Echo voice assistant can broadcast messages to its speakers without consent in situations where, for example adult children may wish to talk to elderly parents. Amazon has been particularly active in this category, buying smart doorbell companies Blink in 2017 for $90 million and Ring in 2018 for $1 billion (Rao, 2019). The company's strategy is centred on what some analysts are calling 'in-home retail', where, combined with smart door locks, Amazon has access to customer's homes for delivering packages more securely. Image recognition technology and AI is also being developed by Facebook for its Portal video service and Google for its Clips offering, which can identify individuals to personalise the information it gives them.
>
> Health sensors. While voice assistants and video monitors can be useful tools to track the activities of vulnerable people in a household, more sophisticated sensors are being developed to monitor for signs of illness. In 2018, Google patented technology for always-on optical sensors that can be placed in household items such as mirrors to collect data on cardiovascular health. In the same year Amazon was granted a patent to detect 'abnormal' voice

conditions such as coughing or sore throats via its Alexa devices (Rao, 2019). While these are still in development, it is possible to imagine them being connected to health providers or relatives wanting to keep an eye on loved ones. The creative ways that data collected in the home for one purpose can be reused for another is illustrated by an initiative from Amazon's ecobee smart thermostat, which can track the movement of individuals around the house. This data is primarily used to more efficiently heat rooms which people use most but can also detect changes in behaviour; ecobee asks it customers to 'donate' their data for use in social projects including one that explores if smart homes could replace retirement homes as data is used to monitor elderly residents. The project is led by Plinio Morita of the University of Waterloo, who wishes to use the data from ecobee thermostats to better understand human behaviour.

For example if an elderly family member begins neglecting the second floor of a home, only making their way upstairs in the morning and at night when they usually go up and down multiple times a day, then this could be a sign of a physical ailment preventing their ease of movement. If a loved one usually frequents every room at home but begins only entering necessary spaces like the bedroom and bathroom, then this could be a symptom of social isolation, and signal a shift in their mental health.

(ecobee, 2018)

Smart vacuum cleaners. This is one of the smaller niches in the smart home category but is interesting in the way the data generated can be used for a variety of purposes. The primary purpose of such cleaners is to save time as they can be set to roam about the house, cleaning as they go. However, in the course of cleaning and avoiding obstacles, the machines collect data about where objects are placed and the size and layout of rooms. iRobot's Roomba device builds maps of the house which allow users to create custom cleaning schedules or instruct the machine to clean specific rooms. In 2018 Google announced a partnership with iRobot to make better use of these maps, to locate products such as Wi-Fi-connected lighting and assign names and locations to lights in different rooms (Vincent, 2018). This data could also be useful for estate agents when a house is sold or let and as an input into home improvement projects and decorating. The partnership fits well with Google's mission statement to organise the world's information and has echoes of its core business over the previous 20 years of indexing the Web for its search engine.

The above are some of the major smart home product categories and illustrate how the data they generate has value to a range of stakeholders. As smart devices take hold in the home, more innovative uses will be found for this data. Some of the sectors with a particular interest in accessing smart home data include:

90 Pervasive computing and data futures

Insurance. Just as the insurance industry has been an active user of telematics data from cars for a number of years, more recently it has been investigating how it can do the same in the home. Insurers are focused on measuring risk to calculate premiums and rely on data to do this. From smart home devices this could include, for example information that water is running in a household even though nobody is at home, signalling a leak. It could be data from smoke detectors on people smoking in the home, room occupancy or the location of major appliances, indicating particular risks. More obvious use cases come from security systems and whether occupants have secured the home correctly and in line with their insurance policy. There are clear issues of privacy in terms of this data and would require home owners to grant access to it by the insurer. However, as with automotive insurance, incentives can be offered in the form of lower premiums if access is granted.

Police. There are obvious reasons why police forces might want access to video feeds from smart doorbells and surveillance systems. Amazon's Ring smart doorbell system, used by hundreds of thousands of households in the US, is already sharing this information via the associated Neighbors app. Throughout 2019, Ring partnered with hundreds of US law enforcement agencies, offering them access to its platform. This has benefits for householders in that the police have a better understanding of illegal activities in their areas but is does raise questions around whether we are building a state-surveillance system that can reach into our home and how closely private companies should be involved in police activities.

Utilities. The data from smart meters helps providers better understand how customers use their energy services. Consumers can also use the data to monitor which devices are using the most energy. Traditionally meter readings are a historical record of what energy has been used while a smart meter tracks in real time consumption patterns. This allows utilities to more efficiently load-balance their networks and offer incentives to customers to switch energy-intensive devices on or off at particular times. An interesting power struggle is emerging between utility power providers and big tech firms as they seek to control this data. Smart meters are traditionally installed and managed by utilities in most countries but as home devices become smarter and new products such as smart plugs and thermostats are launched by Google and Amazon, control is shifting to the technology sector.

Just as Google did with search and Facebook with social media, it is possible that the gatekeeping for smart home data will rest with several companies and others will have to pay to access it. As consumers migrate from screens and keyboards to control much of their technology and associated services, so the companies that built their empires in the age of the PC and the smartphone are trying to remain relevant in this emerging digital world. They will require strategies and business models that can capture and harness data from smart home devices if they are to avoid being marginalised. However, it will also require cooperation over central issues such as security protocols, data protection, data formats and transmission protocols. The internet works as a fundamental underpinning technology because it uses open, non-proprietary standards. Google and Apple control the smartphone market because they developed systems that were closed enough from them to control their evolution and stability but open enough to encourage third-party developers to build apps to sit on top of them. The technologies underpinning many smart home devices are still evolving but it seems clear that a high degree of cooperation over technical standards will be required if users are to fully embrace these technologies. The announcement in late 2019 that Google, Apple and Amazon were going to work together on their Connected Home over IP Project to make these devices work better together is a sign of this (Mihalcik, 2019).

The IoT in our cities

By 2050, 68% of the world's population will be living in urban areas, up from 55% in 2018 (United Nations, 2018). This means an extra 2.5 billion will reside in cities, creating massive challenges for transport, clean air and water, food supplies, energy and housing. Most of this growth will take place in Asia and Africa, with a predicted rise of 43 megacities containing more than 10 million people each by 2030 (United Nations, 2018). Many of these cities are being developed in areas struggling to cope with large human populations due to flooding risks and lack of natural resources and climate change will only exacerbate the problem. Surat in India is a good example of the problems faced by rapid rises in urban population. The city grew from 2.4 million inhabitants in 2001 to 6.6 million in 2018 and is projected to be home to 10 million by 2032 (Parth, 2019). Surat lies at the mouth of the Tapi river, which leaves it prone to flooding. In 2006 floods killed between 150 and 500 people when more than 60% of the city was underwater. Part of the response by national and local authorities in India has been to involve Surat in the country's Smart City initiative where technological solutions are being applied to try and relieve some of the major problems of traffic congestion and energy generation.

While most of the growth in urban areas is taking place in developing economies, there are also increasing pressures on cities in more wealthy countries to make them better places to live. Air quality data for the UK revealed that in 2017, almost 2,000 locations had levels of pollution that exceeded agreed safety limits (Harvey & McIntyre, 2019). The UK government's own health monitoring body revealed that between 28,000 and 36,000 deaths a year could be attributed to long-term exposure to air pollution (Public Health England, 2019). Similar patterns can be found across cities around the world. According to the World Health Organisation, more than 5.5 million people worldwide die prematurely each year as a result of air pollution (Amos, 2016). At the core of these problems are cities with creaking infrastructure and housing, much of which was built in the nineteenth century to deal with smaller populations, different working patters and now-defunct forms of transport. A large part of the solution, many argue, lies with the application of digital technologies and imaginative uses of data. Living and working in and getting about cities of the future can be transformed, it is hoped, by restructuring the systems and infrastructure that could lead to a renaissance for urban living.

Smart cities will be heavily reliant on the widespread distribution of sensors and other data-gathering systems to help local policymakers better understand the most efficient ways to allocate resources. This is the IoT at scale and involves dealing with far greater complexity than making our homes or workplaces 'smart'. Part of the problem is that homes and workplaces are more controlled systems where the devices used to gather data lie within the control of an individual or single company. In cities, there are many more stakeholders spread across public and private organisations as well as the inhabitants themselves. Data formats and transmission protocols are likely to be more diverse and, as a result, incompatible with each other. The data harvested by the sensors is likely to be held in silos, some open but others closed and proprietary to the organisation that collected them. Many citizens will also have concerns about how data is used where it relates to them and who has access to it.

Data is key to the successful running of any smart city with local, national and supra-national governmental bodies as well as academic researchers, think tanks and businesses producing a range of proposals and systems for managing this resource at scale. Emerging solutions tend to rely on a mix of technical and legal inputs to find ways round the messy problems of multiple sources and formats. In the UK, the Open Data Initiative (ODI), a non-profit company that advocates the use of open data, argues that cities need to be seen as ecosystems of people and infrastructure and that data relating to cities also needs to be seen as a dynamic ecosystem. The ODI talks of 'open' cities rather than smart ones and argues that stakeholders need to be brought together to better understand 'where data already exists, where it could be created, and how it could be shared and used' (Thereaux & Wells, 2019). This can be achieved, they claim, through what they call data ecosystem mapping, whereby a visual map is created to show how data is being accessed, used and shared. This approach recognises that many and varied data sources already exist in most cities and that, rather than trying to build a data-driven city from scratch, policymakers and decision makers should start with existing assets. The challenge is to make this data 'discoverable, searchable and actionable in realtime', according to Haque (2016). This, he argues, means leaving the data where it is created and owned and not trying to centralise it into a hub or repository. This has been the approach of many smart city initiatives that draw on current data assets, adding new ones as they emerge and finding innovative ways to combine and add value to these streams. In recent years, some interesting projects and services have emerged that illustrate how many of the pressing problems of modern urban living can be solved or at least alleviated by data.

Traffic congestion

While traffic jams are not the sole cause of pollution, they are a contributing factor as well as a source of stress to those stuck in them. Part of the problem is that personal forms of transport such as the car are not subject to the planning and coordination which governs mass public transport. Millions of individual decisions made each day by drivers as they try to navigate congested streets and traffic management systems designed 100 years ago result in gridlocked streets. Finding ways to monitor traffic flows in real time and adjust routing controls such as traffic lights has been a priority of many smart city initiatives. In the medieval English city of York, networks of sensors have been deployed along the streets to collect data about passing vehicles and change the traffic lights to reduce congestion. The £3-million trial also allows officials to anticipate traffic flows during bad weather and route vehicles through less-busy areas (Bounds, 2018). The sensors are mounted on street lights and other street furniture and track the mobile signals of car drivers so individual vehicles can be tracked as they travel across the city. If successful, the system could be deployed in other cities and will, in the future, be able to communicate with driverless cars.

Air pollution

We know that air pollution is a major killer in cities but building an accurate picture of the levels of contaminants in the air and their composition is difficult due to the hyper-locality of pollution hotspots and the lack of reliable monitoring equipment. Since 2016, Chicago has been part of a project to measure and identify causes of air pollution in the city. A large network of nodes have been placed on lampposts which can measure levels of sulphur dioxide, carbon monoxide, hydrogen sulphide and hydrogen dioxide in real time (Clark, 2017). The nodes are more complex than the sensors typically used to measure air quality and contain up to 15 separate sensors within each of them as well as a computer, two cameras, a microphone and a cooling fan (Thornton, 2018). By May 2018, 100 nodes had been deployed with plans to install a further 400 to complete the project. As well as air quality the sensors are able to monitor temperatures, humidity and vehicle and pedestrian counts via the cameras. The data is then made available freely via either a bulk download or an API that is refreshed every five minutes (AOT, 2019). Developers can then build applications and services on top of this data, with projects including mapping out routes for cyclists and pedestrians to avoid pollution hotspots as they emerge.

Public transport

An important part of any strategy to reduce pollution and congestion is to encourage more travellers onto the public transportation system. Where multiple forms of public transport exist, it can be difficult for users to know which ones to travel on for specific journeys. In London the public body responsible for managing the city's network is Transport for London (TfL). The organisation has made much of its data freely available to third parties with more than 17,000 developers registering to access TfL's APIs, which have powered over 600 travel apps used by

94 Pervasive computing and data futures

42% of Londoners as they plan their journeys (TfL, 2019). The consulting firm Deloitte has calculated that the annual economic value generated from the open release of this data by TfL amounts to approximately £130 million (Deloitte, 2017). The apps powered by TfL data help the millions of commuters that travel into and across London each day to access timetable information and alerts on train and bus delays as well as plan journeys that utilise multiple forms of transport.

The quantified self

A common thread linking the different generations of computing technologies has been a reduction in the size of devices coupled with falling prices. Computers have shrunk from room-sized machines to ones that could fit on desks and then in our pockets. The deployment of IoT systems is part of this trend, with low-cost and low-power devices being embedded in everyday objects and around homes, cities and workplaces. Wearable computing should be seen within this context and encompasses fitness trackers, smart watches and smart clothing. Its primary purpose is to collect data about the person wearing it, including metrics on heart rate, movement, temperature and, in more advanced products, blood pressure. The impact of hundreds of millions of people constantly collecting this data and uploading it to central repositories for analysis will be significant in terms of understanding the relationship between lifestyles and health. Rather than using small samples of volunteers for medical research, scientists could have access to entire populations. Combining this information from other sources and applying AI techniques to spot patterns and causal relationships could transform our understanding of the human body and disease.

As the global market for smartphones and PCs matures, wearables have become a rapidly growing segment of the technology sector. It is estimated that 172 million wearables were sold in 2018, with Apple, Xiaomi, Huawei, Fitbit and Samsung dominating the market (IDC, 2019b). By 2023 it is expected that this will have grown to 260 million sales per year in a global market worth $30 billion (CCS Insight, 2019).

From a business perspective, wearables offer the potential for some interesting data-driven business models. Fitness and health data is amongst the most personal and being the company that collects, stores and adds value to that data could lead to much closer relationships between vendors and users than with previous generations of technology. The sensitive nature of this information also presents risks for vendors as breaches in security leading to data losses could be highly damaging both financially and reputationally. Examining how two of the largest tech companies, Google and Apple, are entering this market offers insights into how they view health and lifestyle data as elements of their overall business strategies.

Apple is the leader in the smart watch sector, with an estimated 48% market share in 2019, followed by Samsung (13%), Fitbit (11%) and other manufacturers (28%) (Purcher, 2019). Despite a mixed reception to its first device in 2015, Apple has succeeded in creating and leading a market where consumers are willing to pay up to $800 for a watch, albeit one that does much more than just tell the time. This data-collecting device should be seen as extending the reach of Apple's ecosystem of products and services as well forming a cornerstone of the company's move into the healthcare sector. According to technology analysts CB Insights (2019), the central pillar of Apple's healthcare strategy is its use of the personal health record. This began in 2013 when the company filed a patent for a wellness registry and then with its purchase of personal health record start-up Gliimpse in 2016. In 2018, Apple opened an API for its health records so third parties could use a development kit called HealthKit to import health record data onto their phones. A number of apps including one for a salad chain called Sweetgreen have integrated HealthKit so that, in the case of Sweetgreen, meals ordered via the app are logged on the user's health record (CB Insights, 2019). These initiatives by Apple, along with other projects the company has run to let medical researchers conduct large-scale studies using patients' iPhones, indicate that it is building a healthcare platform. From the perspective of Apple's core business strategy this fits well as the company has used its expanding ecosystem to increase sales of its hardware from laptops and tablets to phones and watches. Apple has some of the highest profit margins in the technology sector due to its premium pricing and clever branding. In 2018, the company made up only 19% of global smartphone sales but took 51% of total revenues and an impressive 87% of all profits in this sector (Bicheno, 2018). The data generated by these devices is vital to this strategy but only insofar as it encourages users to stay within Apple's walled garden of products and services. If their customers' health records become a core part of this approach and there is a reliance on Apple watches, phones and cloud services to collect and store this data then the ecosystem becomes stronger still.

While Apple uses data to drive hardware sales, Google uses data for its own sake by monetising it through the company's advertising platform. Historically, this has made the company highly profitable as the data it used from its search activities was cheap to source and did not require an expensive and complex hardware business to generate income. Google does market some hardware under its Pixel brand, including phones, tablets and laptops, but these do not generate large sales volumes and are primarily to showcase to third-party manufacturers the potential of the Android and Chrome operating systems. The primary purpose of Google's advance into areas such as smartphones and laptops is to ensure its search services remain central to users as they adopt computing devices beyond the traditional PC and web browser. Its attempts to build a wearable operating system, Wear OS, is no different and is an attempt to remain relevant in this new category of portable computing. However, Wear OS watches manufactured by third parties including Samsung have not been as successful as Android is in the smartphone sector. Part of the problem lies with these third parties adding their own layers of functionality over the operating system, resulting in an inconsistent experience for users. As Apple leads the way in smart watch technology and sales, Google has struggled to respond with products or services of its own that appeal to users. This partly explains the company's purchase of fitness tracker maker Fitbit in late 2019 for $2.1 billion, subject to review by US authorities' concerns about the implications for the transfer and use of Fitbit users' health data. The acquisition gives Google access to Fitbit's 28 million users and a well-established hardware business. Google's plan will be to establish its presence in the wearable market as securely as it did with Android, which itself was an acquisition. Although legal requirements in the US and Europe as well as many other regulations place strong restrictions on how the company could use personal health data to sell advertising, it seems likely that Google will find a way to legally incorporate some of this information into its advertising business.

Although watches and fitness trackers form the main part of the smart wearables sector, clothing is also an important component. The global apparel market is estimated to be worth $1.5 trillion in 2020 – almost three times the value of the smartphone sector (O'Connell, 2019). As sensors and computing components become smaller, more powerful and cheaper, a number of companies are incorporating smart technologies into their clothing. So far, much of these efforts have been focused on military clothing and apparel for professional athletes. The relative expense of these products, the higher budgets available for these types of users and the importance they attach to safety and performance makes them ideal testbeds for this new category. Over the coming years we can expect to see these technologies filter down into more everyday clothing, particularly for amateur athletes. Fitness apps such as Strava, Endomondo and MyFitnessPal have been amongst the most popular in the app stores, with tens of millions of consumers regularly using them. The value of such apps and the data they generate was demonstrated in 2013 when the clothing company Under Armour bought MapMyFitness for $150 million in 2013, followed by its acquisition of MyFitnessPal and Endomondo for $560 million in 2015. This can be seen as part of the company's strategy to become a leader in smart clothing for athletes that can measure performance metrics such as heart rate, body temperature and exercise regimes in the way that phones and wearables do now. As the company's CEO stated after the 2015 acquisitions:

> we want to become the daily destination dashboard, aggregating all you want to know about your general fitness, sleep, steps, activity level and, yes, nutrition.

> *(Comstock, 2015)*

Wearables are the next frontier in the personal computing revolution and will see a large number of new entrants, takeovers, acquisitions and bankruptcies before a stable market emerges. Whether smart watches are stepping stones to embedded computing in our clothing or if yet-unspecified ways to capture health data as we go about our lives will be developed, like the IoT more generally, it will be who controls the data that will determine the winners.

Opportunities for business

It is clear that the rapidly expanding set of tools and methods for generating, capturing, analysing and monetising data offers a myriad of opportunities for businesses to exploit. Never has it been so easy to find and process data and then have the channels through which to distribute it. This section explores some of these opportunities and focuses on two broad areas underpinning them: changes to the foundational technologies, including the blockchain and the Web 3.0 stack, and the places where data can be sourced, including open data repositories and data exchanges.

The blockchain has been mentioned in a previous chapter in the context of providing the back-end infrastructure to authenticate data transactions at scale. According to the Merriam-Webster dictionary, the blockchain is:

> a digital database containing information (such as records of financial transactions) that can be simultaneously used and shared within a large decentralized, publicly accessible network.
>
> *(Merriam-Webster, 2019)*

In practice, it is a method by which digital transactions can be recorded, stored and authenticated across a distributed ledger without the need for a single, central record of transactions. For example, under current mainstream banking systems there is a central organisation that records transactions, a bank or credit card issuer. Using blockchain technologies, these transactions will be logged on multiple computers and will be authenticated when a majority of computers on that blockchain agree it is legitimate. This is a simplified description and there are many flavours of blockchain and distributed ledger technology (DLT). However, the key innovation is the distributing of control away from central bodies to the wider internet. A useful analogy is to think of the difference between sending a letter in the post and sending an email. Under traditional postal systems, a central organisation collects letters from mail boxes, takes them to a central sorting office and then delivers them to addressees via couriers. Email, apart from being much faster, does not require a single organisation to transmit and deliver messages. Senders of emails can use multiple ISPs and telecommunications carriers that need have no formal relationship with those used by the receiver. As long as the providers use the common protocols devised for email, such as POP3 and SMTP, the message will get through.

Many people associate the digital currency Bitcoin with the blockchain but this is only one application of the technology. Many companies have been investing heavily in building blockchain applications to serve different sectors and needs. IBM has led a consortium of major stakeholders including Nestle, Walmart and Kroger in developing its Hyperledger technology for managing supply chains and the data that is required in getting goods from factories to retailers. In the financial sector, blockchain-powered security tokens are being developed which represent real-world assets such as company shares and which are less costly and easier to

98 Pervasive computing and data futures

trade than going through central clearing houses such as stock exchanges. These tokens could also be extended to manage the sale of property and other physical assets. Staying within digital environments, non-fungible tokens (NFTs) are being used to ascertain ownership of digital artefacts. A common problem with digital goods is that perfect copies can often be easily and cheaply made in a way that is not possible with physical items. Copying music, for example when it was distributed in vinyl format was difficult for most people. The rise of CDs as a medium made it easier but was still a problem to do at scale. The MP3 format for digitising and compressing music files and the internet as a distribution channel obviously changed that. However, MP3 music files are still fungible in that they are not unique and are interchangeable in a way that a limited-edition vinyl disc with cover artwork signed by the artist is not. Non-fungible tokens are a way of making digital artefacts unique through DLT. In gaming environments, NFTs are being used to authenticate unique digital assets such as virtual land or weapons. CryptoKitties is a game that allows users to trade unique 'digital collectibles' and digital cats created within the game have been known to change hands for up to $170,000 (Varshney, 2018). From a data perspective, it is important to remember that all these transactions using blockchain technologies are built on the exchange of digital data and do not require central bodies to manage them. The lessons learned from CryptoKitties and IBM's Hyperledger as well as the numerous projects run by the financial services sector can be applied to the building of data exchanges where personal, corporate and legal information can be traded in almost frictionless environments.

An emerging set of technologies where DLT and blockchain technologies will play an important part is commonly referred to as the Web 3.0 stack. Web 1.0 technologies can be seen as 'read-only', where users accessed and consumed Web content via a Web browser but had little opportunity to interact with it. The Web 2.0 environment that emerged in the early 2000s is better described as a 'read-write' web where users had more options to interact with content. Social networks such as Facebook, where individuals could post content and comment on others' posts, or Wikipedia, where anyone could edit entries, are good examples. Although using the Web became more interactive during its first 20 years, the underlying architecture changed very little. Websites were still created and managed by central bodies; even Wikipedia has final control over what edits are allowed and the types of content that are acceptable. Web 2.0 social networks, although dynamic places for the sharing of content, are monolithic structures. Facebook encourages members to post updates and connect with other users but it is a commercial entity that tightly controls this data to sell on to advertisers. Web 3.0 is a set of technologies and protocols from which decentralised apps (dApps) can operate utilising a shared data layer that allows users control of their personal data and the ability to move between dApps with little or no switching costs (Wilson, 2018). Within the Web 2.0 environment a user can, depending on where they live, can request to see the information that Facebook or any other social network holds on them but they cannot take this out in a transferable format and load it into a competing platform. These businesses rely on high switching costs of time and complexity to keep users within their walled gardens.

Data formats are proprietary and so even if switching was theoretically easy, it would be far more difficult in practice. There would also be the crucial issue of not being able to take your social graph in terms of your connections to other users with you when you migrate. In a Web 3.0 world, this data would be portable and ownership would reside with the data subject, not the platform owner. These technologies are still under development and will require a major shift in the underlying infrastructure of the Web but, if many of the legal and social issues discussed earlier in this book are to be resolved, they offer enormous potential. Additionally, just as Web 2.0 triggered a new era of innovation on the Web, so Web 3.0 could do the same by creating a more level playing field for new entrants and data portability. A problem for many start-ups building data-driven business models is the control that the tech giants have over personal data. Web 3.0, if it arrives in the form described above, would undermine that control and see personal data flowing more freely in ways controlled by users rather than monopolies.

Before Web 3.0 becomes a reality, it is likely that greater use of open data via public repositories will form the basis for many data-driven innovations. Open data was discussed in Chapters 3 and 4 in the context of the economics of information and legal approaches to managing public data within Europe and the US. In this section we will consider how open data can be a key input to innovation by many businesses and present considerable opportunities for building new revenue streams. A survey of 450 executives from European digital start-ups as well as conventional businesses revealed that 50% had used open data to build a new product or service (EC, 2018b). Research for the European Commission indicates the value of the European data economy to have grown from €285 billion in 2015 to €300 billion in 2016 and the number of data companies to have increased from 129,000 in 2013 to 134,000 in 2016 (EC, 2018a). Additionally, it has been estimated that the economic value of open data to the 28 EU member states was €52 billion in 2018 (EC, 2018b). It is not unreasonable to assume similar benefits for other countries such as the US that have policies of opening up public data for the private sector to commercially exploit. Firms that have used open public data as inputs to their business models include those producing apps and services for home buying and selling, travel planning, business research and bidding for public tenders. For example in the UK Citymapper uses open data to drive its free mobile app which helps users find the fastest and cheapest travel routes across a city. It does by integrating open data from Transport for London (TfL) as well as from sources in the private sector including Google and Apple. Citymapper's general manager has stated the company chose to launch its service in London because of the easy availability of high-quality, open data.

> The exciting thing about what's going on here is that London, and the UK as a whole, is really progressive in terms of embracing open data, which we're quite happy about. Citymapper was created here because of the existence of open data. It's the essential backbone of what we're working on.
>
> (Techworld, 2019)

100 Pervasive computing and data futures

It is also important to note that the public bodies themselves benefit by being able to use data generated within the sector. It has been estimated that by 2020, €1.7 billion will be saved by EU member states through the use of open data in streamlining their operations (Berends et al., 2017).

Finally, the rise of data exchanges facilitating the discovery and purchase of data from open and commercial sources presents another opportunity for businesses to profit from the rise of ubiquitous computing and the IoT. These range from exchanges that provide access to multiple types of data from a range of industries to those serving more specific niches. Farmobile, mentioned earlier in this chapter, does this for the farming community via the sensors it has deployed across farms. The company creates electronic field records (EFRs) that include data on planting dates, commodity, variety, harvest dates, total production, average yield and more (Lawrence, 2019). This data is then sold via the company's exchange to equipment manufacturers, insurers, agronomists and others and represents a revenue stream for the farmers originating the data. Other exchanges target the automobile sector, global shipping industry, insurance brokers and aviation. Data exchanges are at an early stage of development and have yet to demonstrate business models viable in the longer term. However, they represent a logical step in the evolution of the data industry, where greater liquidity is required if data really is going to be the 'new oil'. It took Google several years before it was able to monetise its dominance in internet searching via its ad exchange business. The company created a fluid and highly profitable market in matching the intentions of searchers with the needs of advertisers. Facebook did something similar with its business model by matching the interests of its users with messages from marketers. Data exchanges offer a logical service in terms of matching data sellers with buyers but technical issues surrounding data formats, APIs and ownership rights are still being resolved. There is also an issue of trust for companies building data-driven products using feeds from these exchanges; they need to be certain that data available today will still be available in the future. It will take a few years before confidence amongst purchasers is sufficiently advanced in the more stable exchanges but when this happens we can expect to see a new generation of innovators building products and services on the back of data exchanges.

Challenges for business

The next generation of data-driven services powered by the IoT and pervasive computing presents many opportunities for businesses capable of seizing the opportunities. However, there are also many potential pitfalls for companies that are not able to navigate this emerging digital world. Some of these challenges relate to digital transformation at a generic level and the significant shifts required in company cultures. Others centre on issues of data ownership, shifting power balances between businesses and consumers, data accessibility and technical standards. This section explores these challenges and outlines some of the hurdles that firms will have to overcome.

Digital transformation is a term used widely in the consulting world for organisations wanting to realign their businesses for a digital world. George Westerman, a research scientist at MIT, defines it as:

> a radical rethinking of how an organisation uses technology, people and processes to fundamentally change business performance.
>
> *(Boulton, 2019)*

It is usually applied to established businesses that are facing competition from new entrants that do not have the legacy systems and processes which can slow down innovation and create barriers with the requirements of modern consumers. Some industries struggle more than others to make this transition, with retail being a good example. Native online retailers such as Amazon that do not have the financial and operating burden of managing physical outlets are at an obvious cost advantage over their older competitors. Many high-street retailers are building online offerings but shifting their businesses and culture to this way of working is difficult and the rise in empty shops is the outcome. The use of data to drive these changes is pivotal but before that can happen an organisation needs to embed a data culture within its workforce. Research from McKinsey suggests that building a data analytics programme for its own sake is not sufficient (Diaz et al., 2018). Such initiatives need to emerge from a desire to make better decisions and this requires data to be made available to everyone in the organisation who needs it as well as the tools to manage it. Where this has happened in firms such as Boeing and Maersk there is evidence that new ideas emerge and operating improvements can be made (Diaz et al., 2018). This all requires better data literacy within firms undertaking digital transformation initiatives. In 1987, the economist Robert Solow famously stated, 'You can see the computer age everywhere but in the productivity statistics' (Triplett, 1999). He was referring to the 'productivity paradox' of massive increases in investments in computing technologies by businesses but no accompanying rise in productivity. It is possible that despite the promise of using data to drive innovation, many firms will not be able to benefit from this potential due to the challenges of cultural change and lack of investments in staff training. Research carried out in 2018 showed slow progress amongst large US companies in implementing data-driven strategies despite their large investments (Bean and Davenport, 2019).

Even where an organisation is able to embed a data-driven culture within its workforce, there is still the challenge of having access to the right information. It may be able to source the data it needs internally but often it will have to look outside its business for third-party sources. This might come from some of the sources such as data exchanges or open data repositories described earlier in this chapter. Although the potential sources of external data are rapidly increasing, being able to navigate this dynamic landscape and find the best sources for specific projects requires some distinct skills. Those tasked with procuring data will need to be able to interrogate often complex repositories, judge data quality, understand data formats and how to process them as well as incorporate them with internal sources.

102 Pervasive computing and data futures

Some organisations have created specific roles for these tasks with Gartner referring to these people as 'data curators' (Schatsky et al., 2019). These curators help firms identify and assess relevant data sources which match business requirements. Forrester Research analyst Jennifer Belissent refers to these people as 'data hunters' or 'data scouts' and defines them by their proactive attitude to sourcing information from often unusual places (Davis, 2019). In their study of European IoT data exchanges, Gaglione et al. (2017) argue that data scouts need to be able to navigate through complex and often unclear data descriptions as well as identify trustworthy data sources and understand detailed licensing agreements. IDC terms this emerging sector of data searching and exchange as Data as a Service (DaaS) and sees it as becoming an essential component of the digital economy.

There are clearly challenges for firms as they search for, access and integrate these new data sources from exchanges and other third parties. As Gaglione et al. (2017) point out, understanding some of the licensing agreements associated with external data is a challenge. Data from long-established sources will be more straightforward to incorporate as vendors will have had time to work out robust and acceptable terms of use. However, some of the newly emerging exchanges, particularly those offering IoT data, are still finding their way through these issues. In the US and Europe, it is generally the case that the owner of the IoT device that collected the data also owns the data it produces (Knight, 2018). However, as data is moved between systems and users and has metadata assigned to it and then combined with other datasets, the situation becomes more complex. Part of the problem is ascertaining who has ownership of the different elements of a broader data ecosystem but there are also technical issues around tracking these elements as they move between different stakeholders. If the value from IoT data is to be fully realised, trusted systems will need to be put in place that automatically assign and track usage rights as data is transferred and integrated into products and services. This is happening in the agricultural sector where farmers typically own the data generated by the sensor networks on their farms but farm equipment manufacturers are building agreement systems to enable this data to flow freely into other systems (Knight, 2018). Economies and broader society will benefit most when access to data is fluid and transparent.

It is arguable that machine-generated data is easier to manage from a legal and technical perspective as it is not generally subject to privacy laws and, as non-sentient devices, machines have no interest in monetising data. In the last chapter, we saw that companies are attempting to create markets for the exchange of personal information which would directly reward consumers for sharing their data. Two of the world's most profitable companies, Facebook and Google, have built their business models on selling their users' data to the marketing industry, with some observers claiming that personal data represents a new asset class (Schwab et al., 2011). With these two companies having a combined annual revenue of more than $200 billion in 2019, this is not an unreasonable claim. From a consumer perspective, being financially rewarded for sharing data will not make anyone rich as estimates for the average annual value of personal data generated by internet usage varies from \$25 to \$200 depending on the location (Grone, 2019; Shapiro, 2019). However, should sustainable markets emerge for the trade of such data, this could have a major impact on the business models of the companies currently reliant on it. Facebook, for example had approximately 2.45 billion users at the end of 2019 (Statista, 2020). At a conservative estimate of \$20 per user this would amount to the company having to pay their users \$49 billion, more than double Facebook's 2018 net income (Facebook, 2020). Business models would clearly have to change to accommodate such a development. Consumers may be faced with a choice of continuing to receive such services for free in exchange for their data or be required to pay a subscription if they wished to sell their data.

If the ongoing backlash against some of the technology giants continues and new regulations emerge to redress the imbalance between data subjects and data collectors then these companies will look for new ways to maintain their profits. In the US, persuading politicians is one approach, with Facebook spending \$12.6 million on lobbying in 2018 (Hodgson and Murgia, 2019). In recognition of a changing political climate, the company has called for a global standard on data sharing that should be enforced by regulators. However, some commentators are critical of Facebook's record on data portability where they have made putting data into Facebook often easier than taking it out. Civil liberties group the Electronic Frontier Foundation (EFF) argues that firm action is needed to prevent further abuses like the Cambridge Analytica scandal, such as giving users an easy-to-use tool for exporting all their data and forcing the company to open up its platforms to innovators and competitors (Cyphers and O'Brien, 2018).

Finally, the IoT and pervasive computing presents a growing challenge to manufacturers from the 'servicisation' of products. This refers to the embedding of sensors and communication technologies within products from jet turbines and tractors to bathroom scales and toothbrushes. Not only do these technologies increase functionality from the generate of data but they also create new potential revenue streams. Companies that have traditionally had no ongoing connection with customers once their products have been bought are now able to manage deeper and longer relationships based around this data. In many cases this can change the business models surrounding products. Rolls Royce, for example has fitted its jet engines with sensors for a number of years but has gradually been moving to new revenue models for its customers. The sensor data is used to drive efficiencies and safety in engine maintenance and the company's TotalCare charges customers based on their usage of the engines rather than a fixed up-front price (Microsoft, 2018). With a Boeing 787's engines generating an average of 500GB of data per flight from the embedded sensors and Rolls Royce monitoring more than 4,500 engines, there is plenty of opportunity to add value for customers (Choudhury and Mortleman, 2018). Other industrial giants including Bosch, GE and Siemens are also investing heavily in making many of their products 'smart' and building platforms for managing the data at the same time. Offering clients the tools to analyse and inform decision making with their data is becoming a core element of many industries products. It also helps lock customers into the firm's ecosystems in

104 Pervasive computing and data futures

much the same way that Apple has done for its consumers. For companies such as Bosch and GE that have the expertise and financial resources to develop services around their product ranges, the IoT presents exciting possibilities. However, there are many industrial firms that will struggle to adapt to this emerging environment. They risk being shut out of the digitisation of the physical world and their products becoming obsolete. As customers realise the benefits of using this data to improve their competitive positions in the market they will increasingly demand their suppliers' products offer digital service elements.

Consumer markets are also facing similar challenges with the rise of the smart home and wearables described earlier in this chapter. In the last ten years, the smartphone has made entire product categories almost redundant, including calculators, personal digital assistants (PDAs), still and video cameras, alarm clocks, portable music players and even torches. Television manufacturers have had to adapt to the demand for smart TVs and rapidly learn about software development cycles and internet security. Toymakers have incorporated internet connectivity and interactive capabilities into their products, with Mattel launching its Hello Barbie doll in 2015 that listened and responded in real time to whoever was playing with it. The product was controversial as it uploaded users' voices to a third-party AI system for analysis and to generate responses. Consumers understandably became concerned that their children's conversations, and even their own, were being recorded and stored on remote servers. However, as voice assistants have become established in many households since 2015, consumer resistance to such devices is reducing. As with many legacy industrial companies, consumer demand for smarter products is challenging many firms to innovate in areas they are not familiar with. It is likely that the 2020s will see a number of high-profile companies struggle to cope in the rapidly evolving data-driven world with the winners being those that invest now in building the skills and knowledge to operate under the new rules of competition.

References

Ali, A. (2018). *Hitachi: The Lumada IoT Platform*. Analysys Mason.

Amos, J. (2016, February 13). Polluted Air 'Causes 5.5m Deaths a Year'. BBC News. www.bbc.com/news/science-environment-35568249.

AOT (2019). API of Things: The official API of the Array of Things Project. https://api.arrayofthings.org/.

Ashton, K. (2009). That 'Internet of Things' Thing. *RFiD Journal, 22*(7), 97–114.

Atluri, V., Baig, A. & Rao, S. (2018). *Tech-Enabled Transformation: The Trillion-Dollar Opportunity for Industrials*. McKinsey & Company.

Bean, R. & Davenport, T. H. (2019, February 5). Companies Are Failing in Their Efforts to Become Data-Driven. *Harvard Business Review*. https://hbr.org/2019/02/companies-are-failing-in-their-efforts-to-become-data-driven.

Berends, J., Carrara, W. & Radu, C. (2017). *The Economic Benefits of Open Data* (Analytical Report 9). European Data Portal.

Bicheno, S. (2018, February 15). Apple iPhone: 19% of Shipments, 51% of Revenue, 87% of Profit [Text]. Telecoms.Com. https://telecoms.com/487806/apple-iphone-19-of-shipments-51-of-revenue-87-of-profit/.

Bloede, K. (2017). *The Industrial Internet of Things.* Woodside Capital Partners.

Boulton, C. (2019, May 31). What is Digital Transformation? A Necessary Disruption. CIO. www.cio.com/article/3211428/what-is-digital-transformation-a-necessary-disruption.html.

Bounds, A. (2018, April 17). York Turns to Technology in Congestion Battle. *Financial Times.* www.ft.com/content/60e758a0-417a-11e8-93cf-67ac3a6482fd.

CB Insights (2015). *Analyzing the Internet of Things Investment Landscape.* CB Insights.

CB Insights (2019). *Apple in Healthcare.* CB Insights.

CCS Insight (2019, March 20). Optimistic Outlook for Wearables. www.ccsinsight.com/press/company-news/optimistic-outlook-for-wearables/.

Choudhury, A. & Mortleman, J. (2018, January). How IoT is Turning Rolls-Royce Into a Data-Fuelled Business. i-CIO. www.i-cio.com/innovation/internet-of-things/item/how-iot-is-turning-rolls-royce-into-a-data-fuelled-business.

Clark, J. (2017, November 7). Big Data, Pollution and the IoT. IBM IoT Blog. www.ibm.com/blogs/internet-of-things/iot-pollution-initiatives/.

Comstock, J. (2015, February 6). In-Depth: Under Armour's Fitness App Acquisition Spree. MobiHealthNews. www.mobihealthnews.com/40365/in-depth-under-armours-fitness-app-acquisition-spree.

Cyphers, B. & O'Brien, D. (2018, July 24). Facing Facebook: Data Portability and Interoperability Are Anti-Monopoly Medicine. Electronic Frontier Foundation. www.eff.org/deeplinks/2018/07/facing-facebook-data-portability-and-interoperability-are-anti-monopoly-medicine.

Davis, J. (2019, May 13). Data Hunter: The New Sexy Technology Job. InformationWeek. www.informationweek.com/big-data/ai-machine-learning/data-hunter-the-new-sexy-technology-job/d/d-id/1334664.

Deloitte (2017). Assessing the Value of TfL's Open Data and Digital Partnerships. Deloitte. http://content.tfl.gov.uk/deloitte-report-tfl-open-data.pdf.

Diaz, A., Rowshankish, K. & Saleh, T. (2018). Why Data Culture Matters. *McKinsey Quarterly,* 3, 37–53.

EC (2018a). *EVALUATION – Proposal for a Directive of the European Parliament and of the Council on the Re-Use of Public Sector Information* (SWD(2018) 145 final). European Commission.

EC (2018b). *IMPACT ASSESSMENT – Proposal for a Directive of the European Parliament and of the Council on the Re-Use of Public Sector Information* (SWD(2018) 127 final). European Commission.

ecobee (2018, April 18). Can Smart Homes Replace Retirement Homes? www.ecobee.com/2018/04/can-smart-homes-replace-retirement-homes/.

Ericsson (2019, November 20). IoT Connections Outlook. www.ericsson.com/en/mobility-report/reports/november-2019/iot-connections-outlook.

Facebook (2020). Facebook – Financials. https://investor.fb.com/financials/default.aspx.

Foster, L.E. (1965). *Telemetry Systems.* John Wiley & Sons.

Gaglione, A., Capossele, A., Puschmann, D. & Gluhak, A. (2017). *SynchroniCity: Delivering an IoT enabled Digital Single Market for Europe and Beyond.* European Union. https://european-iot-pilots.eu/project/synchronicity/.

Gartner (2016). IT Glossary. www.gartner.com/it-glossary/internet-of-things/.

Gold, J. (2019, October 11). How the Oil and Gas Industry Exploits IoT. Network World. www.networkworld.com/article/3445204/how-the-oil-and-gas-industry-exploits-iot.html.

Grone, F. (2019, February 19). Tomorrow's Data Heroes. Strategy+Business. www.strategy-business.com/article/Tomorrows-Data-Heroes?gko=7b095.

106 Pervasive computing and data futures

Haque, U. (2016). Showcase: 'London/Cambridge Cycling' – Finding & Accessing Cross-Domain Urban IoT Data.Thingful Blog. https://blog.thingful.net/post/149362243876/showcase-londoncambridge-cycling-finding.

Harvey, F. & McIntyre, N. (2019, February 27). Pollution Map Reveals Unsafe Air Quality at Almost 2,000 UK Sites. *The Guardian.* www.theguardian.com/environment/2019/feb/27/pollution-map-reveals-unsafe-air-quality-at-almost-2000-uk-sites.

Hille, K. (2018, December 10). Taiwan's Rice Farmers Use Big Data to Cope with Climate Change. *Financial Times.* www.ft.com/content/9f5438fa-ee2d-11e8-89c8-d36339d835c0.

Hodgson, C. & Murgia, M. (2019, September 4). Facebook Calls for New Global Standard on Data Sharing. *Financial Times.* www.ft.com/content/334ab05e-ce64-11e9-99a4-b5ded7a7fe3f.

IDC (2019a, January 3). IDC Forecasts Worldwide Spending on the Internet of Things to Reach $745 Billion in 2019. IDC: The Premier Global Market Intelligence Company. www.idc.com/getdoc.jsp?containerId=prUS44596319.

IDC (2019b, March 5). IDC Reports Strong Growth in the Worldwide Wearables Market. IDC: The Premier Global Market Intelligence Company. www.idc.com/getdoc.jsp?containerId=prUS44901819

Janzen, T. (2019, July 25). Will Carbon Farming Finally Show Us the Value of Ag Data? Precision Farming Dealer. www.precisionfarmingdealer.com/articles/3974-will-carbon-farming-finally-show-us-the-value-of-ag-data.

Kellmereit, D. & Obodovski, D. (2013). *The Silent Intelligence – The Internet of Things* (1st edn). DND Ventures.

Knight, D. (2018, November 12).Who Owns the Data Generated by Machines? Association of Equipment Manufacturers. www.aem.org/news/who-owns-the-data-generated-by-machines/.

Lawrence, C. (2019, March 28). How Data Monetization Is Creating a New Data Economy for IoT – DZone IoT. DZone. https://dzone.com/articles/how-data-monetization-is-creating-a-new-data-econo.

Loizos, C. (2018). Corvus Insurance Lands a Fresh $10 Million to Turn Sensor Data into Actionable Info for its Food and Pharma Customers. TechCrunch. http://social.techcrunch.com/2018/11/26/corvus-insurance-lands-a-fresh-8-million-to-turn-sensor-data-into-actionable-info-for-its-food-and-pharma-customers/.

Mayo-Wells, W.J. (1963). The Origins of Space Telemetry. *Technology and Culture,* 4(4), 499–514.

Merriam-Webster (2019). Definition of 'Blockchain'. www.merriam-webster.com/dictionary/blockchain.

Microsoft (2018). Rolls-Royce and Microsoft Collaborate to Create New Digital Capabilities. Microsoft Customers Stories. https://customers.microsoft.com/en-us/story/rollsroycestory.

Mihalcik, C. (2019, December 18). Apple, Amazon, Google, Others Want to Create a New Standard for Smart Home Tech. CNET. www.cnet.com/news/apple-amazon-google-and-others-want-to-create-a-new-standard-for-smart-home-tech/.

Moon, M. (2015, September 7). BP's Oil Rigs Just Got their Own Internet of Things. Engadget. www.engadget.com/2015/07/09/bp-oil-well-ge-predix-software/.

O'Connell, L. (2019, August 13). Global Apparel Market – Statistics & Facts. Statista. www.statista.com/topics/5091/apparel-market-worldwide/.

Parth, M.N. (2019, February 5). 'We Have to Learn to Live with Floods': Waterlogged Surat to Become Latest Megacity. *The Guardian.* www.theguardian.com/cities/2019/feb/05/we-have-to-learn-to-live-with-floods-waterlogged-surat-to-become-latest-megacity.

Public Health England (2019, March 11). Public Health England Publishes Air Pollution Evidence Review. GOV.UK. www.gov.uk/government/news/public-health-england-publishes-air-pollution-evidence-review.

Purcher, J. (2019, November 8). Apple Watch Market Share Grew in Q3, Delivering More Than 3.5 Times Second Place Samsung. Patently Apple. www.patentlyapple.com/patently-apple/2019/11/apple-watch-market-share-grew-in-q3-delivering-more-than-35-times-second-place-samsung.html.

Rao, M. (2019). *Big Tech in the Smart Home*. CB Insights.

Schatsky, D., Camhi, J. & Muraskin, C. (2019). *Data Ecosystems: How Third-Party Information Can Enhance Data Analytics*. Deloitte.

Schwab, K. (2016). *The Fourth Industrial Revolution*. World Economic Forum.

Schwab, K., Marcus, A., Oyola, J., Hoffmann, W. & Luzi, M. (2011). *Personal Data: The Emergence of a New Asset Class*. World Economic Forum.

Shapiro, R.J. (2019, July 12). What Your Data Is Really Worth to Facebook. *Washington Monthly, July/August 2019*. https://washingtonmonthly.com/magazine/july-august-2019/what-your-data-is-really-worth-to-facebook/.

Siemens (2019). MindSphere: The Cloud-Based, Open IoT Operating. Siemens.com Global Website. https://new.siemens.com/global/en/products/software/mindsphere.html.

Statista (2020). Facebook Users Worldwide 2019. Statista. www.statista.com/statistics/264810/number-of-monthly-active-facebook-users-worldwide/.

Techworld (2019, December 4). Innovative UK Companies Using and Sharing Open Data. www.techworld.com/picture-gallery/startups/-innovative-uk-companies-using-open-data-3613884/.

TfL (2019). Open Data Policy. Transport for London. www.tfl.gov.uk/info-for/open-data-users/open-data-policy.

Thereaux, O. & Wells, P. (2019, May 7). How to Understand and Monitor a City Data Ecosystem to Help Make Better Decisions. ODI. https://theodi.org/article/how-to-understand-and-monitor-a-city-data-ecosystem-to-help-make-better-decisions/.

Thornton, S. (2018, January 2). A Guide to Chicago's Array of Things Initiative. Data-Smart City Solutions. https://datasmart.ash.harvard.edu/news/article/a-guide-to-chicagos-array-of-things-initiative-1190.

Triplett, J.E. (1999). The Solow Productivity Paradox: What Do Computers Do to Productivity? *The Canadian Journal of Economics, 32*(2), 309–334.

United Nations (2018, May 16). 68% of the World Population Projected to Live in Urban Areas by 2050, Says UN. United Nations Department of Economic and Social Affairs. www.un.org/development/desa/en/news/population/2018-revision-of-world-urbanization-prospects.html.

Varshney, N. (2018, September 5). Someone Paid $170,000 for the Most Expensive CryptoKitty ever. The Next Web. https://thenextweb.com/hardfork/2018/09/05/most-expensive-cryptokitty/.

Vincent, J. (2018, October 31). Google Wants to Improve your Smart Home with iRobot's Room Maps. The Verge. www.theverge.com/2018/10/31/18041876/google-irobot-smart-home-spatial-data-mapping-collaboration.

Wholey, M. (2019). *Agtech and the Connected Farm*. CB Insights.

Wilson, F. (2018, July 11). The Web 3 Stack. AVC. https://avc.com/2018/07/the-web-3-stack/?utm_source=feedburner&utm_medium=feed&utm_campaign=Feed%3A+AVc+%28A+VC%29.

Wodark, J. (2017). *Data-Driven Opportunities in the Smart Home and Implications for Insurers*. Verisk Insurance Services.

7
CONCLUSION

We have seen that data in all its forms, from clay tablets to web pages, has been primarily driven by the needs of business, the desire to make profits and the requirements of governments to raise taxes. Where money or goods are exchanged, records need to be kept, ownership ascertained and taxes paid. The evolution of the data industry is characterised by greater volumes, faster distribution and easier reproduction. The computing age has only accelerated these trends. Since the first stock exchanges started trading shares and commodities, data has been used as a source of competitive advantage, from Reuter's pigeons in the nineteenth century to Spread Network's $300-million fibre-optic cable in 2010.

However, as the preceding chapters have shown there is more to competing with data than simply getting it before your competitors. What you do with the data is often more important than how much you have or how quickly you can access it. In many sectors, data is a commodity available to everyone so companies need to be innovative in their management of it. Before Google, search engines struggled to build sustainable business models around the activity of their users. Google established a highly efficient marketing engine that matched what users wanted to know with advertisers' needs for relevant audiences. The company transformed what had been seen as an almost worthless by-product of internet searching into a multi-billion-dollar and highly profitable business. Facebook did something similar with users' social graphs. Data is a unique commodity in that it can be distributed and replicated at almost zero cost and be re-used multiple times without degrading its quality. This allows new business models to emerge and rewrites many of the rules of competition. Until the twenty-first century, business success was often based on scarcity of resources with the winners being those that controlled the physical assets. In a digital world, the most valuable companies are those that control the data and the platforms it resides in.

110 Conclusion

The rise of digital platforms and the business models that have emerged from them will dominate many commercial sectors in the 2020s. The first sectors to be impacted by the digital revolution have been the more information-intensive, such as media and entertainment and financial services. We are now seeing more industrial sectors such as transport, utilities and manufacturing incorporating digital technologies and workflows and making use of the data that flows from these changes. As ML and AI is applied to these datasets we can expect to see more rapid and extreme changes to the competitive environments they operate in. As recent research from Stanford University has shown, between 2017 and 2019 the time required to train a large image classification system fell from 3 hours to 88 seconds (Perrault et al., 2019).

Just as legislators in the US broke up some of the largest industrial companies in the twentieth century, so regulatory pressures are being brought to bear on some of the digital giants of today. The concern is the scale of the data these companies hold and the highly personal and sensitive nature of much of it. Despite claims made by many companies holding records of our online activities that it is all anonymised, we have seen that it takes very little to link much of the data to named individuals. A recent investigation by *The New York Times* demonstrated how easy it was to access the movements of millions of mobile phone users around the US via a digital marketing company that quietly sells this data on to interested parties.

> To evaluate the companies' claims, we turned most of our attention to identifying people in positions of power. With the help of publicly available information, like home addresses, we easily identified and then tracked scores of notables. We followed military officials with security clearances as they drove home at night. We tracked law enforcement officers as they took their kids to school. We watched high-powered lawyers (and their guests) as they travelled from private jets to vacation properties.
>
> *(Thompson and Warzel, 2019)*

It is debatable whether it is too late for regulators to prevent these activities from taking place. Perhaps the genie is out of the bottle and, to judge by our willingness to use the devices and apps that are generating this data, perhaps most people don't really care. Without public pressure for change it is difficult to see elected representatives spending political capital on tackling it. Stricter regulations such as the GDPR in Europe and the California Consumer Privacy Act in the US are steps in that direction but without a firm will to implement them and the necessary resources for those tasked with enforcing them, they may not have a significant impact on business practices. As with many areas of law, the combination of rapidly advancing technologies and nimble business managers makes it almost impossible for legislators to stay ahead of the market.

However, this same ingenuity is also being applied to solving some of the world's most pressing problems with data. A growing global population, dwindling natural resources and climate change demand that the private and public sectors work together to ensure the survival of humanity. Data will play a big part in these endeavours as it can help farmers be more productive, ensure transportation systems operate more efficiently and provide citizens with the information they need to make more informed decisions about their consumption and lifestyles. It is important that data is made more accessible for innovators to build solutions to these problems and that it does not fall into the control of a few large corporations in the same way that that most developed economies for much of the twentieth century were dominated by a small number of industrial giants. The open data movement and the technologies behind the blockchain and Web 3.0 point to the start of a route where data can be harnessed for the greater good and individuals can become more empowered to control their personal data.

References

Perrault, R., Shoham, Y., Brynjolfsson, E., Clark, J., Etchemendy, J., Grosz, B., Lyons, T., Manyika, J., Mishra, S. & Niebles, J.C. (2019). *The AI Index 2019 Annual Report.* Human-Centred AI Institute, Stanford University. https://hai.stanford.edu/sites/g/files/sbiybj10986/f/ai_index_2019_report.pdf.

Thompson, S.A. & Warzel, C. (2019, December 19). Opinion: Twelve Million Phones, One Dataset, Zero Privacy. *The New York Times.* www.nytimes.com/interactive/2019/12/19/opinion/location-tracking-cell-phone.html.

INDEX

Note: Page numbers in *italic* indicate figures on the corresponding pages.

access: to personal information 66–67; to the right information 101–102
advertising: Facebook 35; Google AdWords 26–27; before the internet 31; mass media and marketing, rise of 9–10; monetisation of the internet 30–32; personalised targeting of individuals 31–32; programmatic 31–32; real-time bidding 31–32
Age of Enlightenment 5
aggregators 67–68, 78
agriculture sector 85–86, 102
air pollution 91, 93
Alphabet Inc. *see* Google
Amazon: AI in automated processes 37; differences between big four companies 40–41; ecobee smart thermostat 89; Google and 37; Internet of Things (IoT) 88; Marketplace 37; NHS project with 71–72; origin and growth 36; pillars built on 36; Prime 37; strategy 36–37; as threat to competitors 37
Aneja, S. 16
anonymisation/deanonymisation of personal data 60–61, 68
apparel market 96
Apple: Computers 52–53; differences between big four companies 40–41; evolution to data-centric model 38; Fast Healthcare Interoperability Resources

(FIHR) 39; health data 94–95; iPhones 27, 38; Siri 38–39; smart watch 94–95; Watch 39
apps 28
arbitrage 7–8
ARPANET 22
artificial intelligence 28–29
Ashton, Kevin 83–84
audio systems 57
Australian Competition and Consumer Commission (ACCC) 73
automobile insurance sector 54

Babbage, Charles 11
banking sector 55–56
Battelle, John 26, 27
Belissent, Jennifer 102
Berners-Lee, Tim 22, 30
block printing 4–5
blockchain technologies 74, 97–98
Bloomberg Terminals 49
books, printed 5–6
Bosch 85
Boulton, C. 101
BP 86–87
Braun, J.A. 76–77
breaches of personal data 68
British Airways 68
broadband networks 26
Bush, Vannevar 7
business data sector, growth of 4

114 Index

business models: Business Model Canvas 45–46, *46*; data-driven 47–49; defined 45; emerging data-driven 52–57; financial reward for sharing own data 102–103; importance of as conceptual tool 46; innovation in, impact of 46–47; platform-based 49, 52–57
business opportunities in Internet of Things (IoT) 97–100

Cairncross, Frances 41
Cambridge Analytica 65, 69
Capital One 68
car insurance sector 54
Chandler, Alfred D. 13
Chicago, air pollution in 93
China, TikTok app and 64
choice, customer lock-in and 40
cities, Internet of Things (IoT) in 91–94
Citymapper 99
clothing, smart 96
cloud storage, migration to 17
Code of Hammurabi 3
computing age 11–12
Comstock, J. 96
connected homes 87–91
consumer markets, challenges for 104
copies of data 17
Corvus Insurance 86
costs, fixed/variable, in a data-driven business 51
credit: first known rules for 3–4; growth of 4; information, growth of 8–9
Credit Kudos 56
customer lock-in 40
Cusumano, M.A. 52

dacadoo 55
Darnton, R. 50
data: cloud storage, migration to 17; concerns over use of 39–41; copies of 17; economics of 49–52; and information, definitions 14; knowledge from *14*, 14–15; as national resource 66; as the new oil 15–17; types of 16–17; volumes of 16
data brokers 30, 59–60, 66, 68
data curators 102
data-driven business models 47–49; emerging platform-based 52–57; wearables 94–96
data ecosystem mapping 92
data exchanges 100

data generation as by-product of computing 13–14
data hunters/scouts 17, 102
data strategy models: Amazon 36–37; Apple 38–39; differences between big four 40–41; Facebook 34–36; Google 32–34
data trusts 66
Davis, J. 17
Day, Benjamin 9
deanonymising of personal data 60–61, 68
DeepMind/Royal Free deal 70–71
democratic processes, threat to 69, 77
Desjardins, J. 3–4
development of business data *see* origins and development of business data
digital transformation as challenge 101
digitisation of data 11
direct marketing 10
dotcom crash 25
driverless cars 54

economics of data 49–52
economy, information: cloud storage, migration to 17; copies of data 17; rise of 12–15, *13*, *14*; value of 16; volumes of data 16
Eklund, J.L. 76–77
electronic communications 10–11
Electronic Frontier Foundation (EFF) 103
Encyclopaedia Britannia 50–51
energy services, use of Internet of Things (IoT) 90
EU–US Privacy Shield 64
European Union regulation 62–63
external platform strategy 52–57

Facebook: advertising, targeting of 35; Cambridge Analytica case 69; data exchanges 100; differences between big four companies 40–41; network effects 34–35; origin and growth of 34; social manipulation during elections 36
Farmer's Business Network (FBN) 86
Farmobile 86, 100
fashion sector 56–57
Fast Healthcare Interoperability Resources (FIHR) 39
financial data: banking sector 55–56; credit information 8–9; as profitable market 49; stock exchanges, growth of 7–8
fitness trackers 55, 94–96
fixed costs in a data-driven business 51
football analytics 56

Gaglione, A. 102
Galloway, S. 35, 37
Gawer, A. 52
General Data Protection Regulation (GDPR) 62, 68, 73
General Electric (GE) 85
Goldsmith, C. 73
Google: AdWords 26–27, 31; Amazon and 37; Android phones 33; Android system 53; data exchanges 100; DeepMind/Royal Free deal 70–71; differences between big four companies 40–41; health data 94–95; Home products 34; Maps 34; market share 30; mission of 33; NHS project with 70–71; origins 32; Page Rank algorithm 32–33; wearable market 94–96
governments, recognition of changes 17
Gupta, A. 16
Gutenberg, Johannes 5

Haque, U. 92
Harford, T. 3
health data 29–30, 94–95; Apple Watch 39; Fast Healthcare Interoperability Resources (FIHR) 39; sensors 88–89; sharing of with private sector 69–72
Hern, A. 60
high-value datasets 62–63
Hill, Kashmir 66, 67
history of business data *see* origins and development of business data
Hitachi Insight Group 85
Hodson, H. 71
Hollerith, Herman 11
home, Internet of Things (IoT) in 87–91
Hu, J. 67
hyperscale platforms 54

IDC 16–17
Industrial Revolution 5
Industry 4.0 29
information: and data, definitions 14; knowledge from *14*, 14–15
information economy: cloud storage, migration to 17; copies of data 17; rise of 12–15, *13*, *14*; types of data 16–17; value of 16; volumes of data 16
information management during WWII 7
innovations, impact on economic growth 12–13, *13*
insurance sector 54–55, 86, 90
Intel 52–53
international trade in information 63–64

internet: abundance of information, move to 24–25; Amazon 36–37; Apple 38–39; Apple iPhone 27; apps 28; broadband networks 26; differences between big four companies 40–41; dotcom crash 25; Facebook 34–36; Google 26–27, 32–34; innovation wave 1, 1994–2000 23–25; innovation wave 2, 2000–2007 25–28; innovation wave 3, 2007–2018 28–30; Internet of Things (IoT) 28–29; investment opportunities 23–24; mobile networks 26; mobile phones 27; monetisation of 30–32; Netscape 24; origins of 21–23; programmatic advertising 31–32; rapid growth in users 23; real-time bidding 31–32; rise of 11; smart devices 29–30; smart manufacturing 29; technological revolutions 25–26; Yahoo! 24
Internet of Things (IoT): access to the right information 101–102; agriculture sector 85–86; air pollution 93; business opportunities 97–100; challenges for business 100–104; cities 91–94; clothing, smart 96; consumer markets, challenges for 104; data collection as core purpose of 84; data exchanges 100; data hunters/scouts 102; defined 84; digital transformation as challenge 101; early automated collection of data 84; fitness trackers 94–96; growth of sector 84; health sensors 88–89; home 87–91; increased efficiencies due to 87; insurance sector 86, 90; internet innovation wave 3, 2007–2018 28–29; monitors 88; near-real-time, actionable insights in 87; oil industry 86–87; open data 99–100; origin of term 83; personal data as property to buy and sell 102–103; police, use by 90; public transport 93–94; restructured processes and workflows 87; RFID tags 83–84; servicisation of products as business challenge 103–104; smaller firms, benefits for 87; smart meters 90; smart speakers 88; smart vacuum cleaners 89; traffic congestion 92–93; utilities 90; workplace and industry 85–87

Jefferson, Thomas 50
Jordan, Julius 3

Katz, M.L. 34
Kellmereit, D. 83

116 Index

knowledge from information *14*, 14–15
Kondratiev, Nikolai 12
Kondratiev Waves 12–13, *13*
Korsakov, Semen 11

legal sector 56
legislation *see* regulation
Licklider, J.C.R. 21
life insurance sector 54
lock-in, customer 40
London, public transport in 93–94
Lyft 53

machine learning (ML) 28–29
Machlup, Fritz 13
managerialism 6–7
Marchetti, Federico 56
market research 10
marketing: Facebook 35; Google AdWords
    26–27; mass, rise of 9–10; monetisation
    of the internet 30–32; personalised
    targeting of individuals 31–32; real-time
    bidding 31–32
mass marketing, rise of 9–10
mass media: impact of internet on
    traditional 41; rise of 9–10
Mayhew, F. 41
McDowell, M. 56
McKinsey & Co. 54, 85, 101
media: impact of internet on traditional 41;
    mass, rise of 9–10; value chains 76
medical insurance sector 54–55
Melendez, S. 66
memex machine 7
Merkel, Angela 29
Microsoft 52–53
mobile networks 26
mobile phones 27; Android phones 33;
    apps 28; smartphones 33–34;
    uniqueness of 40
Moll, Joana 60
monetisation of the internet 30–32
Money Dashboard 56

Nadler, A. 77
net neutrality 78–79
Netscape 24
network effects 34–35, 39–40
new firms, data-driven business models
    of 48–49
New York Sun 9
newspapers: advertising in 9; impact of
    internet on 41; mass media, rise of 9–10;
    New York Sun 9; printed 5–6

NHS: Amazon project with 71–72; Google
    project with 70–71
non-fungible tokens (NFTs) 98

Obodovski, D. 83
occupations, creation of new 17
oil industry 86–87
open data 52, 66, 99–100, 101
Open Data Directive (Directive (EU)
    2019/1024) 62–63
Open Data Initiative (ODI) 92
origins and development of business data:
    advertising 9–10; computing age
    11–12; credit system 3–4; devices used
    by businesses 6–7; earliest records 3;
    electronic communications 10–11;
    information economy, rise of 12–15,
    13, *14*; internet, rise of 11; managerialism
    6–7; mass media, rise of 9–10; printing
    presses, rise of 4–6; record keeping
    6–7; stock exchanges, growth of
    7–8; telecommunication networks 11;
    telegraphs 10–11
Orna, E. 62
Osterwalder, A. 45–46, *46*

packet switching 21–22
Pasternak, A. 66
Payment Services Directive 2 (PSD2) 55
Perez, Carlota 25
personal data: interest in changing markets
    for 74–75; as property to buy and sell
    73–74, 102–103
personalised targeting of individuals 31–32
pervasive computing *see* Internet of
    Things (IoT)
Pigneur, Y. 45–46, *46*
platform-based business models 49,
    52–57, 78
police, use of Internet of Things
    (IoT) by 90
political manipulation via data
    misuse 69, 77
population of urban areas 91
Porat, M.U. 13–14
Powles, J. 71
printing presses, rise of 4–6
privacy: anonymity of personal data 60–61;
    health data, sharing of 69–72; history of
    regulation 61–63; international trade in
    information 63–64; niche uses of data 57;
    personal data as property to buy and sell
    73–74; regulation 110
programmatic advertising 31–32

Index   117

public information, access to 61–63
public-sector bodies, data generated by 51–52
public transport 93–94

radio advertising 9–10
Ram, A. 40
Rayward, W.B. 5
re-use of public sector information (RPSI) 62–63
real-time bidding 31–32
Reardon, Joel 40
record keeping 6–7
regulation: access to personal information 66–67; aggregators 67–68; aims of 78; anonymisation/deanonymisation 68; changing nature of digital businesses 67; current models 63–64; data brokers 59–60; EU 62–63; future for 76–79; health data, sharing of 69–72; high-value datasets 62–63; history of 61–63; informed position, policymakers need to take 77–78; international trade in information 63–64; limits of 64–68; need for 59–61; net neutrality 78–79; privacy 110; re-use of public sector information (RPSI) 62–63; recent cases 68–72; recent rulings and proposals 72–75
Reinsel, D. 16
reliance on businesses of data 17
Reuter, Paul Julius 8
revolutions, technological 25–26
RFID tags 83–84
ride-hailing apps 53–54
risk management and understanding 86
Robinson, Richard 69
robotic vacuum cleaners 57, 89
Rocher, L. 68

Safe Harbor Principles 64
Schoffer, Peter 5
Schumpeter, Joseph 12
scientific management 6–7
Scism, L. 55
Second World War, information management during 7
servicisation of products as business challenge 103–104
Shapiro, C. 34, 50, 51
Shapiro, R. 16
Shepardson, D. 79
Siemens 85
Sift 66
Siri 38–39

small firms, data-driven business models of 48
smart clothing 96
smart devices 29–30
smart homes 87–91
smart manufacturing 29
smart meters 90
smart speakers 88
smart vacuum cleaners 89
smartphones 28, 33–34, 40
Smith, A. 12
Solow, Robert 101
SpaceXs Starlink project 8
speed of technology adoption 15
sporting data 56
Spread Networks 8
stock exchanges, growth of 7–8
Surveillance Capitalism 65

Taiwan 86
taxi services 53–54
Taylor, F.W. 6
technological revolutions 25–26
technology adoption, speed of 15
Teece, D.J. 45, 46
telecommunication networks 11
telegraphs 10–11
television advertising 9–10
Tennison, J. 66
Tett, G. 69
Thirani, V. 16
Thompson, Ben 67–68, 78
Thompson, S.A. 110
TikTok app 64
time and motion studies 6
tipping 75
traditional sectors, use of data by 48
traffic congestion 92–93
transformation, digital, as challenge 101
transnational trade in information 63–64
Transport for London (TfL) 93–94

Uber 53
ubiquitous computing see Internet of Things (IoT)
Underwood, Barbara 79
urban areas, Internet of Things (IoT) in 91–94
user-generated content 51
utilities, use of Internet of Things (IoT) 90

vacuum cleaners, robotic 57, 89
value chains 76

118 Index

variable costs in a data-driven business 51
Varian, H.R. 50, 51
volumes of data 16

Wanamaker, John 27
Warzel, C. 110
Waters, R. 75
Watson Healy, L. 16
wearables 94–96
Web 3.0 stack 98–99
Westerman, George 101
Wikipedia 51
Wolfe, J. 57

World War II, information management
   during 7
World Wide Web: origins of 21–23; *see also*
   internet
Wunderman, Lester 10

Yahoo! 24
YNAP 56–57
York, Internet of Things (IoT) and 92–93

Zittrain, Jonathan 22
Zuboff, S. 65
Zweig, J. 10